IRONDAD

A Midlife Crisis in 140.6 Miles

Authors:

Darren Gibbons & Alan Adye-Rowe

IRONDAD: A Midlife Crisis in 140.6 Miles
© **2025 Darren Gibbons** & **Alan Adye-Rowe**

First published in Great Britain in 2025

The right of Darren Gibbons and Alan Adye-Rowe to be identified as the authors of this work has been asserted in accordance with the UK Copyright, Designs and Patents Act 1988.

If you can't be fast, be funny.

— Darren Gibbons

Marginal gains, maximal giggles.

— Alan Adye-Rowe

It started with bin bags. It rarely ends with sense.

— Ian Dawson

Table of Contents

Prologue

This isn't a training plan. It's a field report from a man who once believed that "a long day out" meant two coffees, one biscuit, and the brief but noble walk to the car.

I'm not the poster boy; I'm the warning label. The fine print that says results may vary, batteries not included, do not attempt without adult supervision. My progress is measured in unhelpful units — effort in stubbornness, speed in "audible wheezing," and recovery in the number of stairs it takes before my legs file a grievance.

Technology disapproves of me. My watch vibrates in disappointment. My scales sigh when I approach. My running shoes, once a cheerful orange, now resemble props from a forensic documentary. My legs are older than my ambitions and unionised against me.

At home, I live under a benevolent dictatorship. My wife specialises in calm sentences that can end a crusade at fifty paces. My children specialise in repeating those sentences back to me with improved punctuation. They form the official Board of Caution — I propose new adventures, they respond with the kind of silence usually reserved for bad medical news. Occasionally, a plan is approved, on the strict understanding that I won't end up in traction or trending locally.

What follows in these pages is the honest version of "getting fit" — the one that smells faintly of regret and Deep Heat. It features wardrobe malfunctions engineered by hubris, etiquette errors that should be criminal, and nutritional experiments that would make a lab rat lawyer up. There are moments of glory so small they'd need a microscope, and failures large enough to qualify as infrastructure.

There are spreadsheets with the moral authority of the tax office, snacks chosen with the strategic brilliance of a raccoon, and training alarms that sound suspiciously like regret. Most days start with optimism and end with ibuprofen.

I promise three things.

First: I'll tell the truth about effort. Not the glossy cinematic montage sort, but the kind where you find yourself negotiating with gravity and your own cardiovascular system. The kind where one minute lasts an eternity, and the victory is not quitting, despite having fifty perfectly good reasons to.

Second: I'll keep explanations short and the jokes slightly too long — mostly because I need the rest. If there's a technique, I'll misunderstand it. If there's a mistake, I'll refine it into an art form. If there's equipment, I'll assemble it upside down, swear creatively, and call it a "stress test."

Third: I won't pretend I did it alone. There are volunteers in this story — friends who mock me into perseverance, family who perform quiet miracles of patience, and strangers who cheer for reasons I don't fully understand. They're the unsung heroes keeping me from quitting and, more importantly, from dying stupidly.

Every ridiculous endeavour reaches a point where you stop and realise you've gone far beyond the jurisdiction of common sense. If this book has a destination, it's that moment — reached slowly, expensively, and with a pocket full of receipts for items that promised "elite performance" and delivered chafing.

There are no spoilers here. No triumphant finish-line scenes, no glossy medal selfies, no sentimental soundtrack swelling in the background. Just this quiet truth: somewhere between "maybe" and "what the hell am I doing," a person can change shape in ways mirrors will never show. Patience thickens. Pride shrinks. The world expands slightly, usually while you're gasping for breath and regretting lunch.

If you're here for perfection, there are manuals for that — glossy, instructional, and featuring people who don't sweat like they're being interrogated.

If you're here for company — for the honest, absurd, occasionally catastrophic attempt to do something that terrifies you just enough to make you feel alive — then pull up a chair.

Tighten the straps. Check nothing important is on backwards.

Right then. On we go

PART 1: The Click That Changed Everything

Chapter 1: Bin Liners and Bad Decisions

It is a truth universally acknowledged that a middle-aged man in possession of a mortgage must be in want of a bad idea.
Mine began, as all catastrophes inevitably do, with bin liners. Not a bar brawl, not a chance encounter with a cult, not even a suspicious late-night text from a colleague named "Shaz" — no, my personal doomsday clock was set ticking by a family-pack of lemon-scented 30-litre drawstring bags and a veiled threat from my wife that the kitchen was beginning to resemble the final days of Rome.

Connie — my wife, eternal taskmaster, and human incarnation of a productivity app — had instructed, not asked, that I "finally deal with the kitchen bin situation before it becomes a public health hazard."
"Deal with it today before it becomes a Category Three biohazard" she'd said, while wielding a pair of Marigolds like surgical gauntlets.

Connie doesn't nag — she orchestrates. She delegates. Her to-do lists have footnotes. Her footnotes have cross-referenced appendices. She once labelled the dishwasher as a "Cutlery Sanitisation Compartment" and also once scheduled a deep-clean of the airing cupboard and referred to it as a "Quarterly Fabric Storage Review."

She tidies the way a mafia accountant audits the books — precisely, unforgivingly, and with the unspoken threat of cement shoes for non-compliance. She doesn't yell. She tightens Tupperware lids with a vengeance that makes your testicles retract. She has a sixth sense for rogue socks and unemptied bins and, most terrifyingly, can detect the misuse of her 'good scissors' despite being in another postcode.

And she's always right. Tragically, relentlessly right. Which, as any married man will tell you, is infinitely worse than being wrong.

There I was, hunched at the kitchen table in a hoodie that hadn't seen a wash since the Six Nations, eyes narrowed at my laptop screen, locked in a life-or-death struggle over whether to purchase the reinforced drawstring Citrus-Fresh elite liners or the cheap-as-sawdust ones that split faster than the Tory party.

Jack, my youngest, eight years old and currently possessed by the spirit of a deranged snack-based arms dealer, was launching spoonfuls of cereal at the dog with the precision of a military drone operator.

He wasn't eating. No. He was conducting a live experiment in food ballistics. Bella, our long-suffering spaniel — a creature so lazy she once fell asleep mid-bark — was sat with mouth open, vacuuming Cheerio's out of the air like a hairy Pac-Man with no self-respect.

I told him to stop. He grinned the grin of a boy who knew full well I had no authority, no energy, and no back-up plan.

Upstairs, the teenager lurked.

Ellie — fifteen, hormonal, and more emotionally unstable than a pigeon trapped in a conservatory — was brooding in her scented lair. She communicated solely in sighs, slamming doors like a haunted but disinterested poltergeist. Her bedroom door had become a kind of emotional Morse code.
One slam: mildly miffed.
Two slams: I'd dared to exist within 500 metres.
Three slams: I'd committed a war crime such as speaking in public and I was on thin ice for existing.
Earlier in the week, she asked me to drive her to school "so I don't arrive looking like I've survived a medieval uprising." I said no. She retaliated by calling me "vintage" in a tone that suggested I was woven from asbestos and irrelevance.

Meanwhile, Connie had begun muttering ominously. Words like "feral" and "standards" escaped from the sink zone where she scrubbed a saucepan with such force I suspect she was removing fingerprints — possibly mine.

***

And me?
I was online.
For the fifth time this week. Shopping. For bin bags.

This, I thought — this was manhood's quiet descent. Not crashing, not burning, but gently evaporating into algorithm-approved purchases and existential despair.
I've been a car mechanic since I was nineteen. I know how engines work. I understand torque ratios and drive shafts. And yet, when it comes to my own life? I am a man with no manual and a very squeaky fan belt.

There had been dreams, once. Grand ones. But somewhere between nappy changes, leaky sheds, and trying to find matching socks during a school morning apocalypse, those dreams packed their things, left a note, and vanished into the night.
Now? My biggest thrill was whether Amazon Prime could deliver compost caddies before lunchtime.

I rubbed my temples. One task, I thought. One click. One bin-related triumph.
And then it happened.

Right there, sandwiched between a promotion for biodegradable liners and a vitamin D supplement targeting men with early-onset decrepitude:
IRONMAN WALES – ARE YOU TOUGH ENOUGH?

140.6 Miles. One Day. Swim. Bike. Run. No Excuses.

I should have laughed. Closed the tab. Returned to the soothing embrace of drawstring density specifications.

Instead, I clicked it.
Fool.

The screen flickered. And then came the music.

Epic, thunderous, the sort of music that usually accompanies divine judgement or shampoo commercials for men with majestic hair.
Bella startled. Jack dropped a spoon. I mashed the mute button and grabbed my headphones like I was accessing classified adult content.

The first scene: a man — heroic, dripping — sprinting into the ocean with the urgency of someone late to a war or escaping a stag do gone terribly wrong.

Cut to: a legion of neoprene-clad gladiators on a windswept Welsh beach, all square jaws and stoic gazes, like the audition line-up for a Russell Crowe gladiator remake.

Then cyclists, scaling hills that would make goats weep. A grinning pensioner, salty and magnificent, rode like he'd found spiritual enlightenment halfway up a 12% incline and was now daring you to try the same.

***

The music swelled. The drama mounted.

And then came the pièce de résistance — a woman, broken but victorious, stumbling over the finish line like she'd survived battle, childbirth, and possibly leg amputation. Volunteers caught her like she'd just escaped a collapsing building in an action film. She collapsed into the arms of a child and wept — joy, pain, maybe dehydration. Possibly all three.

And then the voice. Deep. Biblical. A voice that sounded like it had once narrated plagues:
"This is not a race. This... is your reckoning."

My reckoning?
Mate, I was shopping for bin liners.

But I watched the whole thing. Every glorious, manipulative second.
It got me. Not in a "tearful awakening" way — more in the same

vein a cheesy movie gets you when you're hungover, bloated, and emotionally fragile.

Maybe it was the music.
Maybe it was the bloke who looked like Gandalf, if Gandalf had a gym membership.
Maybe it was the simple fact that I hadn't done anything impressive since I parallel-parked outside Greggs in one attempt last Tuesday.

But the idea — the stupid, ridiculous, flatulent idea — it took root.

What if I did something like that?

Not seriously, obviously. I didn't own a wetsuit. My bike had been consumed by the shed during the early Brexit years. And the last time I'd run anywhere was to catch the recycling truck with a wine bottle I was too ashamed to admit was mine.

I glanced across the kitchen. Connie's abandoned foam roller sat untouched — a cursed artefact from the brief Pilates Renaissance of 2022. It was now a reminder that we were a family of triers... who didn't.

And yet, the thought remained. Lurking.
Festering.
Plotting.

The screen changed.
Secure your spot today. Balance due later. Deferrals available.

Even the call to action sounded like a polite mugging.
Come. Suffer.

My mouse hovered.
I should have walked away. Returned to the citrus-scented safety of my to-do list.
Instead...

Click.
Name. Email. Emergency contact.
Yes, I accept the possibility of injury, public nudity, and

spontaneous loss of dignity.
And there it was:

WELCOME TO IRONMAN WALES, IAN DAWSON.

I stared. Long and hard.
Bella stared back. Her expression said, you've done something idiotic again, haven't you?
She wasn't wrong.

This is how it starts, I thought.
Not with a plan. Not with a purpose.
But with bin liners.
And a very, very bad decision.

Chapter 2: Welcome to IRONMAN

I approached IRONMAN training the way one might approach a blinking warning light on the dashboard: with wild optimism, dangerous underqualification, and the faint hope it might go away if I just turned the stereo up. I expected to find something straightforward, like "go outside and jog until you're thin" What I found was more like someone had poured treacle into the engine and told me to just "believe in myself" while driving uphill.

Zones. So many zones. Heart rate zones. Training zones. FTP zones. Lactate threshold zones. It was less like an exercise plan and more like I'd accidentally enrolled in a military coup in the Matrix.

There were diagrams. There were acronyms. There were sentences like "maintain Zone 2 effort until your glycogen stores deplete, then switch to MAF protocol." I am a man who rebuilds engines for a living and even I couldn't follow half of it. One online forum ended its advice with the phrase "HTFU." I had to look it up. It means "Harden The F*** Up." Marvellous. Next time someone asks how to change a tyre, I'll just shout "Toughen up!" and lob them a spanner.

It was as if I'd asked the internet, "How do I run a marathon?" and been handed a horse, a javelin, and a tight deadline.

Naturally, I did what any overwhelmed man does when life becomes too much: I grabbed the dog lead and exited the house under the guise of "fresh air" and "taking a moment" but in truth I just wanted to hide behind the dog and pretend I hadn't just sold my future dignity for £499 and an ill-timed impulse click.

Bella, my spaniel and constant witness to my midlife demise, bounced beside me cheerfully, entirely unaware that her owner had just signed up to exercise recreationally for seventeen hours or die trying in front of thousands of people while dressed like a latex-wrapped goose.

We headed down toward the Porthcawl seafront. It was overcast in that classic British way — the sky was the shade of unresolved arguments, and the sea had the look of something recently inconvenienced. Somewhere out there, where I definitely can't touch the bottom — physically or emotionally. I was supposed to swim on purpose. Among people who foam-rolled for fun and had thighs that didn't chafe.

I stopped at the railings near Rest Bay, hands in pockets, and contemplated the endless expanse of churning water like a 19th-century poet staring into his own failure. I was expected to swim in that. On purpose. With people who considered compression socks a fashion statement and knew what "cadence" meant outside of the Royal Marines.

My brain — ever the drama queen — staged an entire cinematic sequence of my future demise:

Race day. The horn blasts. Everyone charges forward like Norse warriors storming Lindisfarne. I sort of shuffle, wheezing from the effort of walking across the sand. My goggles fog. My foot cramps. I am overtaken by what may or may not be an inflatable flamingo being used as a floatation device for a child. A lifeguard begins paddling toward me with the same expression one reserves for rescuing a capsized llama. He waves. I wave back. It's less "thanks" and more "tell my wife I died doing something stupid."

And then — the bike.

Technically, I own one. It's in the shed. Or under the shed. Or possibly is the shed now, having fused with the surrounding debris during a particularly aggressive windstorm. My imagined ride involves Baz's old mountain bike, last used to fetch lager and a distressed firework from Aldi. I am overtaken by everyone: elderly people with baskets, children with stabilisers, a man dressed as a carrot for climate justice. Every incline becomes Everest in disguise. By mile sixty, I've dismounted and am sat in a bush re-evaluating my life choices and googling "can you get a refund for trauma."

And then, the pièce de résistance: the marathon.

At this point, every part of me hurts. My knees have applied for early retirement. My nipples feel like I've been rubbing them with wire wool dipped in vinegar. I am overtaken by someone juggling. A marshal yells "You're doing great!" and I respond with the haunted smile of a man who is actively hallucinating a kebab. At one point I think I see a bath. Then the Virgin Mary. Then a Greggs. I begin weeping gently, but stylishly.

I shook my head.

No. No, this was lunacy. Me? A man whose exercise regime was "take two trips from the car so I don't spill the shopping." I am not an athlete. I'm just a bloke with creaky knees and a takeaway loyalty card. I'm a second-hand engine with too many miles, questionable wiring, and a service history written in crayon.

This, I told myself, was the moment to cancel. To claim fraud. To say it was the dog. Or blame Connie. Or Mark Zuckerberg.

But I didn't.

Bella sniffed a bin, sneezed with deep moral judgement, and carried on walking as if her owner wasn't actively sabotaging his musculoskeletal system.

I trudged past the arcade, past kiosks selling sun cream in February and fishing nets in monsoons. A group of teenagers stood vaping under a NO SMOKING sign with the confidence of young men who have never pulled a muscle sneezing. One wore sliders with socks. In January. The youth of today fear nothing. Not laws. Not frostbite. Not future joint pain.

I stopped to check my phone. The email was still there. No typos. No escape clauses. No line that said, "Just kidding, we do this to middle-aged men for fun."

WELCOME TO IRONMAN WALES, IAN DAWSON.

It didn't read like a welcome. It read like the terms and conditions of a duel at dawn.

And then there was Dan.

My oldest friend, chief enabler, and patron saint of bad decisions. If I ever murdered someone in a moment of passion, he'd be the one digging the hole and asking if we could stop for chips on the way. We'd met decades ago stacking tyres in a garage that smelt permanently of petrol and Pot Noodles. Dan had a beard back then too — claimed it was "iconic", though it looked like he'd glued a ferret to his chin with mayonnaise.

He once attempted a half-marathon dressed as a pint of Guinness. Collapsed at mile seven and declared he'd "done enough to earn the medal emotionally."

I imagined telling him. I could already hear the laughter. That breathless, hiccupy, near-asthmatic cackle that ends with tears and usually a pulled muscle.

***

Back home, I slipped off my shoes, de-leashed Bella, and stood for a moment, one hand resting on the dining chair, like a Regency gentleman debating whether to duel or run away screaming.

Upstairs, Connie was deep in her quarterly wardrobe cull — I could hear the drawers opening and closing like artillery fire. Once she reached that level of domestic war footing, you stayed low and out of sight. She'd already banished three mismatched socks and a pair of sandals that "no longer reflected our values."

I opened the laptop. The bin liners were still in the basket, staring at me like loyal employees awaiting instruction. But I ignored them. I had bigger problems now.

I opened Excel.

Because if I was going to implode, I'd do it with colour-coding.

IRONMAN TRAINING PLAN – MASTER FILE

Under that, I typed:

Monday: Research

Tuesday: Rest (from research trauma)

Wednesday: Jog? Possibly chase the dog.

Thursday: Core (if lower back not in open revolt)

Friday: Pub (for morale)

Saturday: Turbo? (Find out what this is)

Sunday: Brick? (Definitely not masonry?)

Then I created a motivational header:

GOALS:

Do not die

Finish with at least one toenail

Avoid public vomiting

Look vaguely athletic at least once

Prevent wetsuit from becoming an instrument of humiliation

I then made the foolish mistake of going on YouTube.

The first video: "IRONMAN TRAINING FOR COMPLETE BEGINNERS." The man on the thumbnail had the abs of a Greek statue and the eyes of someone who'd seen the Devil on the bike leg.

He began with: "If you're thinking of signing up for IRONMAN... don't."

Thank you, "IronDean85". If only I'd met you 36 minutes earlier.

Another video: "What's In My IRONMAN Race Day Bag?" The woman began unpacking like she was heading to survive on a remote island, revealing gels, powders, lubricants, spare socks, talc, and what appeared to be a military-grade torch.

Just then, my phone buzzed. Dan.

Dan: Pub tomorrow still on, or are you still barred after the darts trophy incident?

Me: Still on. Got something to tell you.

Dan: You're not dying, are you? Or worse — giving up bacon?

Me: Worse.

Dan: You've joined a pyramid scheme.

Me: IRONMAN.

Dan: Like the Avenger?

Me: No. Triathlon. Swim. Bike. Run. In Wales.

Dan: SWEET HELL. Who did this to you?

Me: I did. Voluntarily. Kind of.

Dan: I'm buying the first pint. I need to see the exact moment your brain explodes trying to explain this.

I put the phone down.

Bella licked my leg — either comfort or an attempt to taste-test me in case I died and left her to forage.

I stood. Stretched. Pulled something.

Classic.

I sat again, the way one sits after a hernia and a minor betrayal. My spreadsheet blinked at me. The confirmation email loomed.

And somewhere beneath the sarcasm and the spreadsheets, a tiny voice asked:
What if this isn't about IRONMAN?

What if it's about proving I haven't completely rusted?

That underneath the Dad jokes, the biscuit belly, and the unmatched socks...
There's still someone in there worth rebuilding.

God help us all.

Chapter 3: "You Signed Up for What?"

Where the silent treatment hits DEFCON 3 and one man realises he may have destroyed his marriage over a pair of Lycra shorts.

There's something deeply unsettling about a silent kitchen. Especially when you're married. It's not the peace of contentment—it's the ominous hush of a battlefield before the cannon fire. The air itself felt like it was plotting. It hung heavy, like the moment just before a school nativity play goes horribly wrong—when you know disaster is coming, but all you can do is brace for a child in a donkey costume to vomit on the Virgin Mary.

The kitchen table offered no comfort. Just a few stale crumbs, a coffee so cold it had entered a new state of matter, and the creeping suspicion that somewhere nearby, a woman was about to begin a quiet and devastating inquisition.

The bin had grown to such proportions it had developed edges. It now had corners, structural integrity, and an ominous lean. Meanwhile, Jack had gone to school looking like he'd been styled by a blender full of muesli, and Ellie—the teenage storm cloud—had muttered "whatever" at a piece of toast and vanished in a fragrant gust of contempt.

The laptop screen glowed with the sort of digital smugness usually reserved for automated parking fines.

WELCOME TO IRONMAN WALES, IAN DAWSON.

It radiated pride, like it had just enlisted me in a noble quest instead of a glorified torture circuit involving neoprene, road rash, and the public humiliation of waddling like a duck in cleats.

Tabs flicked back and forth in vain. Maybe the confirmation email had somehow un-sent itself. Maybe the IRONMAN website had collapsed under the weight of middle-aged regret.

Maybe I'd hallucinated it all during a carbohydrate-induced fugue state.

The email was still there. Mocking. Unapologetic. Glowing like a neon sign over a pub toilet: ABANDON HOPE, ALL WHO CLICKED HERE.

The delete button tempted briefly, as if denying it would somehow unwrite history. But the cosmic mistake had already occurred. The universe had registered it. A tribunal of athletic demigods had laughed.

Bella, the dog, raised her head, stretched like a retired gymnast, and gave me a look that combined pity, concern, and the faint scent of judgement. Not angry. Just quietly disappointed, like she knew I shouldn't be trusted near keyboards—or kettles.

I clicked back to the shopping tab. The bin liners I'd originally meant to buy were still in the basket, blinking like confused orphans. "We were your purpose," they seemed to say. "You've betrayed us for Lycra."

Upstairs, floorboards creaked. The tell-tale tread of slippers moved with the kind of careful deliberation that only spelled trouble. Too soft to be casual. Too casual to be innocent.

The footsteps reached the kitchen just as the laptop closed— not quickly enough.

Connie entered, laundry basket perched like a throne on one hip, eyes scanning the room like a military drone. The recycling received a frown. The coffee got a raised brow. Then her gaze landed on me, and a soft, barely perceptible pause descended. Not anger. Not yet. Just the deeply intelligent calm of someone preparing to deliver consequences.

"What's IRONMAN Wales?"

She'd seen it. Of course she had.

"You left the tab open."

No yelling. No theatrics. Just weaponised calm. The kind of calm that lives in the centre of hurricanes and every mother's ability to make grown men cry using only a slightly tilted head.

"I was ordering bin liners."

The words floated from my mouth with all the conviction of a man denying paternity on daytime television.

The laundry basket was placed gently onto the counter. Deliberately. As if resisting the urge to throw it directly at my head.

"Is it a cult?"

That was a difficult one. Technically no, but the clothing alone suggested otherwise.

"It's a triathlon."

Eyebrows rose like a pair of perfectly choreographed guillotines.

"As in... swim, bike, run?"

A single nod.

"In the sea?"

Another nod. Smaller and slower this time. The nod of a man who knew he was already neck-deep in metaphorical sewage.

She folded her arms. This was not casual body language. This was the loading sequence for a verbal missile strike.

"And you paid money for this?"

"There's a deferral policy," I said, as if that would somehow cast a veil of reason over the madness.

"Excellent. Flexible madness."

She exhaled through her nose. Long and controlled. The kind of breath reserved for yoga instructors trying not to scream into a beanbag.

"You haven't run since that sock incident in 2016."

"It was a windy day."

"You pulled your calf chasing a sock."

"It was moving deceptively fast."

She ignored me.

"And the bike?"

"In the shed."

"Right. Probably rusted solid and married to the lawnmower by now?"

"A bit of WD-40 and a whispered prayer. She'll ride again."

She didn't speak. She didn't need to. Her eyebrows did an entire silent TED Talk on the subject of poor decision-making.

"Do you actually think this is a good idea, Ian?"

Then she left. No slamming. No shouting. Just the slow, silent exit of a woman whose husband had made yet another profoundly idiotic life choice.

Two minutes later, Bella re-entered, sniffed the air as if checking for radioactive shame, then resumed her position under the radiator with a sigh.

The laptop reopened itself with the reluctant click of doom.

"do people actually finish IRONMAN Wales or is it a trap"

The search results painted a vivid picture.

One blog post titled "I Cried on All Three Legs" described the event as "type-two fun with a body count."

Another was just a photo of a man wrapped in foil, holding a banana, captioned: NEVER AGAIN.

Someone claimed to have finished in twelve hours and called it "a lovely day out." Either he was lying or suffering from a concussion.

The swim? Described as a "full-contact washing machine" and "saltwater MMA."

The bike? "Hilly enough to make you question the shape of the Earth." "Relentless." "Designed by the ghost of a sadistic goat."

The run? "Like watching a zombie parade staged in a sauna." "You will cry. Accept this early."

What began as curiosity rapidly devolved into psychological erosion. By midday I had consumed three race-day vlogs, watched a man unbox a wetsuit while weeping gently, and eaten two bananas for reasons unknown even to myself.

YouTube recommended a video titled IRONMAN TRAINING FOR ABSOLUTE BEGINNERS. The presenter was smiling too much and clearly hadn't blinked since Brexit.

"Let's talk base-load efficiency!"

The tab was closed instantly.

Next: a sample training plan.

Monday: Swim – 1hr

Tuesday: Bike – 90 mins

Wednesday: Run – 10 miles

Thursday: Strength & mobility

Friday: Recovery spin

Saturday: Long ride – 3 hrs

Sunday: Brick session

It read like an ancient punishment ritual. I needed a plan that began with "Can jog to the fridge without collapsing."

I retreated to the safety of a video titled Funny Triathlon Fails Compilation. Ten minutes of people faceplanting into barriers, being attacked by swans, and mistaking the bike mount line for a rest stop. I laughed so hard I nearly woke the dog.

Back to the spreadsheet.

Title:
IRONMAN TRAINING PLAN – MASTER FILE
Subheading: Death, Lycra and Bananas.

This week's schedule updated:

Monday: Watch fail videos

Tuesday: Google "brick" (still not convinced it's real)

Wednesday: Consider jog (briefly)

Thursday: Ice knees from thought of jogging

Friday: Emotional strategy session (at pub)

Saturday: Window-shop for turbo trainers

Sunday: Cry. Watch montage. Eat biscuits.

A new tab: KEY TARGETS

Don't die

Avoid wetsuit-related disgrace

Convince Connie this isn't a breakdown

Learn what cadence is

Actually buy the bin liners

Phone buzzed.

Ellie:

"Mum says you've lost it. Don't drag us into your Lycra spiral. Also, can I have £10 (not snacks)."

Then Baz:

"Dan says you've entered a death race? Should I dig a grave now or wait till your bloated body washes up near Barry Island?"

Another message followed:

"P.S. You can borrow my daughter's bike. It's pink. Says 'Princess Sparkle'. Take it or leave it."

At this point, I'd have accepted a scooter shaped like a baguette.

Back to the spreadsheet. Risk levels colour-coded:

Green: Probably fine

Orange: Questionable

Red: May require medical intervention

A new tab: INSPIRATION

One guy did IRONMAN on every continent

One woman breastfed while running

One bloke did the whole race in a Big Bird costume

All clearly unwell

Bolded Friday's "Pub" session and underlined it twice. Just in case.

The phone buzzed one more time.

Dan:

"Still breathing? Or have the Lycra overlords claimed your soul?"

The spreadsheet blinked innocently. The email sat like a goblin on my shoulder.

One final entry was added:

Top Target: Lie Confidently About Progress. Especially When Drinking.

Chapter 4: Training Begins at the Bar

In which training is attempted, friendships are tested, and every man present should really know better.

The Dog & Towel was the kind of pub where the wallpaper had long since surrendered, the air was 38% chip fat, and the carpet had so thoroughly absorbed the souls of past patrons that stepping on it felt like walking on regret. It smelled like stale beer, wet dogs, and decisions that would haunt you in therapy. The kind of place where hope came to die quietly behind the fruit machine.

Dan was already seated in our usual spot—the back wall, just beneath the radiator that hadn't functioned since 2003 and now served only to drip faintly when it rained, like a guilty conscience. He had his pint in hand and the smirk of a man who knew, without being told, that someone close to him had committed an act of staggering stupidity.

He raised his glass by way of greeting. "Still banned from darts night, then?"

I sighed, already exhausted. "Temporarily. It was a misunderstanding."

"You stood up to give an acceptance speech."

"I was being supportive."

"For spectating."

"I was caught in the moment."

"You thanked the brewery, the town of Porthcawl, and 'all who believe in pub-based excellence.'"

"It was a strong cider."

Dan nodded solemnly, like a doctor reviewing your X-ray and seeing nothing but flaming bin fires. "And now this."

I peeled off my coat like a man removing a bandage from a wound he inflicted on himself. "I've signed up for an IRONMAN."

Dan blinked. Once. Slowly. Like a man processing the sentence "I've adopted a crocodile" or "I've started a mime troupe."

"To confirm—the race? Not the Marvel one with the flying suit? The one where grown men weep in wetsuits and call it a lifestyle?"

I nodded. The nod of a condemned man who's accepted his fate, but would still like to lodge a complaint with management.

Dan's face moved through the emotional gears of confusion, amusement, pity, and finally unfiltered glee. He took a long, slow, sip of his pint with the satisfaction of a man watching a friend voluntarily set himself on fire.

"You've lost your entire mind."

"I'm doing something meaningful."

He raised one hand. "Objection. You cried during the Bake Off final last year because the baker dropped their roulade. You are not emotionally qualified to endure mild wind, let alone an endurance event."

"I'm building up to it."

"You're building up to a hernia."

"I needed a challenge."

"You needed therapy. Or a puzzle. Or a rock garden. Not a three-part death march followed by a t-shirt as the reward."

I pulled out my notebook.

Dan recoiled as if I'd revealed a contagious rash. "Oh no. You've got a log."

"It's structured."

"It's symptomatic."

I handed it over. Dan opened it like it might bite.

Monday – Think about training
Tuesday – Stretch (mentally)
Wednesday – Maybe a jog
Thursday – YouTube 'how to turbo'
Friday – Pub (strategic carb load)
Saturday – Panic and try a brick
Sunday – Apologise to family

Dan stared at the page like it was written in crayon by a nervous wombat.

"This is a breakdown. In calendar format."

"It's a starting point."

"It reads like the diary of a man who counts bin day as cardio."

A sudden series of thuds interrupted us. THWACK. THWACK. THWACK.

Sandra—local darts assassin, legendary drinker, and the only woman in Porthcawl legally categorised as a weapon—was mid-match. She was hurling darts with the same controlled fury she used to respond to neighbourhood Facebook threads about dog fouling.

She was playing solo. Judging by her expression, she was losing to herself—and still not pleased.

Dan nodded toward her without moving his lips. "She knows."

"Knows what?"

"About you. Connie told Karen. Karen told Sandra. Sandra told the council. You're officially 'that IRONMAN bloke.'"

Sandra hit a triple twenty, drained her pint, and marched past us without so much as a wobble. As she passed, she muttered, "Triathlon, eh? We'll save you a seat. You'll be back by June."

Then disappeared into the toilets like a dart-wielding banshee.

Dan leaned in, whispering with the reverence normally reserved for ghost stories. "We should all be more like her. Dangerous, and hydrated."

He sat back. "Let me get this straight. You willingly signed up to drown a bit, cycle until your knees issue a formal protest, and then run until you start seeing sounds?"

"That's the gist."

"You don't own a wetsuit, your bike is essentially a decorative shrub, and your last known run ended in a limp and a kebab."

"That's why I'm easing in."

"You're easing into oblivion."

I sipped my pint. It tasted of barley, poor judgement, and distant future physiotherapy bills.

Dan grabbed a napkin and began scribbling.

Monday – Panic
Tuesday – Regret
Wednesday – Google 'foam roller'
Thursday – Cry during stretch
Friday – Pint
Saturday – Shout at YouTube coach
Sunday – Reassess all life choices

He slid it across the table. "Stick that on your fridge."

"This is deeply unhelpful."

"It's a map. A map of your descent into Lycra-induced madness."

"I used to be sporty."

"You once lost a race to a toddler. Who was crawling."

At that exact moment, as if summoned by mockery, Baz and Kev exploded into the pub like the budget version of Ant & Dec—if Ant had a neck tattoo and Dec once got suspended for pushing a teacher into a bush.

Baz entered first, waving a folded betting sheet like he'd just cracked a Cold War code. We'd known each other since sixth form, where we bonded over bad decisions, poor academic performance, and a shared allergy to logic.

Kev followed, already grinning like he'd been practising the face all day. Kev was built like a wardrobe, lived for amateur football, and delivered every sentence like it was both an insult and a sermon. He once got a red card in a charity match for aggressively tackling a nun.

Baz slapped the betting sheet on the table with the excitement of a child who's found explosives.

Kev pointed at me. "It's true! You've joined the Lycra cult!"

Baz beamed. "I've got twenty on you never leaving the swim. Kev reckons the changeover bit will finish you off—whatever it's called. He thinks tri-suits are a form of psychological warfare."

Kev added, "I've seen soufflés with better muscle tone. You'll cramp before you even get wet."

"I'm not going to cramp."

Dan raised a hand. "You once cramped tying your shoelace."

"Isolated incident."

Kev sat down like gravity owed him money. "Let's break this down. You're doing a full IRONMAN?"

"Yes."

"Swim. Bike. Run."

"Yes."

"All in one go?"

"That is generally how it works."

Kev blinked, as if seeing me for the first time. "You've lost your actual mind."

Baz leaned forward, adopting the tone of a condescending PE teacher. "What's your FTP?"

"My what?"

Kev groaned and did that thing where he covered his eyes like he was shielding them from my stupidity.

"Functional Threshold Power," Baz said, in a voice that suggested he'd read two articles and now considered himself a coach. "It's like an MOT for your legs. And you're currently operating at advisory levels with one wing mirror and no clutch."

"If you were a car," Kev added, "you'd be a Vauxhall Corsa with five warning lights, two flat tyres and a boot full of takeaway wrappers."

Baz clapped me on the back. "Don't worry. We'll tow you over the finish line. Might even strap a GoPro to you for documentary purposes."

Kev narrowed his eyes. "Do you even have a bike?"

"In the shed."

"Still in one piece?"

"More or less. It might be dating the lawnmower."

"Tyres?"

"Spiritually flat."

"Frame?"

"Structurally... adjacent to usable."

Baz snorted. "So essentially a garden sculpture with pedals."

"I'll sort it."

"Will you also sort your cardiovascular system? Or are you planning to borrow one?"

They spent the next fifteen minutes subjecting me to an interrogation so intense it may have breached the Geneva Convention. Kev asked how much chafing cream was too much. Baz googled "how to prepare for death by triathlon." At one point, they tried to estimate my VO_2 max using a beer mat and a packet of crisps.

Eventually, they wandered off to play pool and argue about whether peanut butter counts as a protein supplement.

Dan turned to me. "You've made my entire month."

He took a sip. "I know it's mad. But oddly? It suits you. You versus a thousand Lycra-clad lunatics. You're like a Shakespearean tragedy in running shoes."

We sat in silence for a moment.

Dan broke it with a question. "So when do you buy the tight shorts?"

"I'm building up to them."

"Wise. Rushing Lycra is how marriages end."

Outside, Porthcawl glistened with the sheen of a town that knew better. The stars twinkled overhead with the knowing smirk of celestial beings who'd seen this sort of thing before.

***

At home, the kitchen felt colder. Bella looked up from her blanket with the solemn expression of a dog who'd been left out of a will. I stood for a moment, coat in hand, staring at nothing.

Not in a reflective, philosophical way. I just genuinely didn't know what the hell I was supposed to do next.

Eventually, I opened the laptop. A tab was already open.

Triathlon Essentials.

I stared at it.

Then typed:

"how to swim when you haven't swum since... whenever."

Because apparently, the IRONMAN swim is in open water. Not a nice warm pool. Not a leisure centre with floaties and a lifeguard called Barry. The sea. A giant, freezing soup of salt, feet, and primal fear.

And I'm supposed to enter it. Voluntarily. Wearing neoprene. With strangers. All flailing like caffeinated eels at a Black Friday sale.

My IRONMAN journey so far:

Confessed in pub

Mocked by friends

Judged by a darts champion

Threatened by wife

Achieved precisely nothing except mild indigestion

And the worst part?

Now it's real.

Because once the lads knew, it was no longer a passing fancy. It wasn't "something I might do." It was "that thing Ian's doing," and they were invested in exactly the same way Roman crowds were invested in the lion pit.

Kev had already renamed the group chat to "Ironmess."

Baz was asking if he could ride in the support car with snacks and a megaphone.

Dan had said, "We believe in you," with the tone of a man placing a bet he expected to lose.

Now I had to go through with it.

Or leave the country.

Interlude: Where Ambition Meets Crisps

It's Saturday. According to the gospel of triathlon, I should be swimming, cycling, or running—or, at the very least, being chased by something large and angry in lycra.

Instead, I am horizontal. Draped across the sofa like a Renaissance painting of emotional collapse. I'm wearing a dressing gown last washed during the Olympics (London), one sock that keeps trying to escape, and an expression that says, "I've been through things."

At my side: an empty tub of hummus I swear I didn't intend to finish. It started as a casual dip. Now it's a crime scene.

Bella is on the rug, paws in the air, snoring like she's auditioning for the role of "sleeping walrus #3" in a Channel 5 nature documentary. She looks like she's boycotting the concept of effort.

I reach for my phone, the modern man's portal to self-esteem erosion, and type into Google:

"How to train for IRONMAN without losing marriage, job, or sanity"

I am rewarded with 6,000 results, a mild heart murmur, and a rising sense that triathlon is just a polite way of saying "early grave, now with branded water bottles."

Close phone. Eat more hummus.

I flick through Instagram. Naturally, "IronDean85" is out again, posting something infuriating:

"Recovery run (only 20k) #GrindNeverStops"

Only 20K. I briefly consider phoning the authorities to report him for crimes against humility.

The TV is on mute. Something about elite triathletes. I unmute it just in time to hear a man called Jürgen shout "PAIN IS FUEL!" while charging up a hill using ski poles, two GPS watches and

28

what appears to be internal combustion. His heart monitor beeps with the urgency of a microwave about to explode.

I say to no one in particular, "Where are the biscuits?"

In a moment of accidental productivity, I reach for my training notebook—the one that still smells faintly of desperation—and jot:

WEEKLY REFLECTION
– Still alive
– Legs: technically present
– Mindset: dissolving like cheap gravy
– Training plan: still fictional
– Googled "Can you wing an IRONMAN?" (twice)
– Didn't cry in public (this week)
– Called that progress

I pause. Draw a lightning bolt. Immediately cross it out. It felt too optimistic. Like hope had snuck in through a side window.

Somewhere in my brain, a voice mutters, "You are categorically not built for this." A cruel whisper, probably originating from the same lobe that makes me buy gluten-free granola and then resent it.

But another voice—smaller, stubborn, slightly drunk—says, "Yes, but... you said yes."

I don't get up.

I don't move.

But I think about it. And for today, that counts.

PART 2: Base Building, Bullshitting and Bushes

Chapter 5: Couch to Collapse

There exists a unique moment of dread in the lifecycle of foolish ambition, and it is this: standing by your front door, laces tied, phone strapped to your arm like an underqualified cyborg, convincing yourself that this run—your first run—isn't, in fact, the beginning of a breakdown in four sweaty acts.

I hadn't moved. Not a single heroic stride. Yet I was sweating. Not the noble, endorphin-laced sweat of the accomplished, but the nervous, anticipatory perspiration of a man who has just realised he is about to move his entire body... at pace... on purpose... outdoors.

Bella, sprawled on the hallway rug like a furry panic attack, eyed me with the concern she normally reserved for thunderstorms and the vacuum cleaner. Connie walked past with a laundry basket balanced on one hip, glanced at me without stopping.

"Is this it, then?" she said, the corners of her mouth twitching. "The moment athletic greatness begins?"

"I'm going for a run," I replied, inflating my chest in what I hoped looked like confidence but likely resembled a medical emergency.

She nodded with the slow gravity of someone humouring a man on trial. "And if you don't return, do I tell them it was natural causes or pride-related trauma?"

I stepped outside like a man unsure if the ground would hold. The air greeted me like a damp slap—classic Welsh weather: wet, passive-aggressive, and always loitering with intent.

My joggers clung to my thighs as if fearing abandonment. My hoodie—a veteran of garage clear-outs and failed DIY attempts—had absorbed moisture at the speed of gossip in a small village. I looked less like a runner and more like a discarded uncle at a barbecue who'd wandered too far from the sausages.

The neighbour waved from across the street. I gave a nod best described as legally required. They looked inspired. I looked like a man attempting a sponsored escape.

Phone out. App open. Tap: "Easy Run – 20 minutes."

"Easy," it said. Like it knew nothing of my knees.

I began. Or more accurately, I lurched. A cautious forward hop, like someone testing the loyalty of their own hamstrings. Each step echoed with the squelch of doubt.

I rounded the corner. Picked up the pace. Mistake.

Halfway down the street I was overtaken. Not by another runner. No.

By a toddler.

On a balance bike.

Wearing a Spider-Man helmet.

Singing "Let It Go" with one hand in a bag of Quavers.

He did not acknowledge me. He ghosted me at full pelt, powered by pure carbohydrates and the uncrushable belief that he was, in fact, Spider-Man. I briefly considered a low trip. I didn't do it. Character development.

My lungs, unaccustomed to such antics, began drafting their resignation letters. My calves were sending coded distress signals to my knees. My entire system was falling apart like a flat-pack bookshelf assembled by drunks.

But I kept going.

Because now I had to. Now it was a matter of honour. Or at least inertia.

Ahead: a park bench. A beacon. A promised land of sitting. I staggered towards it like a wounded medieval pilgrim.

I collapsed onto it with the grace of a wardrobe toppling from a delivery van.

Bella, who'd kept a ten-metre buffer like a seasoned health-and-safety officer, ambled over, sniffed, and flopped down with a groan that said, "Tragic, but predictable."

She hadn't been on a lead. She hadn't needed to be. From the moment we left the house, she'd sensed the pointlessness of this expedition and had chosen the noble role of distant observer, like a Royal Family member attending a charity event. She kept a dignified distance, like a bystander watching a man reverse a caravan for the first time — painfully, inevitably, sideways.

I stared at my shoes. They didn't deserve this. They were made for light errands. Maybe some brisk walking around B&Q. Not this farcical re-enactment of athletic effort.

Then, like a cruel joke scripted by the gods of cardio, she arrived.

The jogger.

Real. Efficient. Floating.

Ventilated top. Actual running shoes. Legs sculpted by purpose. She nodded politely as she glided past, entirely unbothered by gravity.

I attempted a nod in return, which may have resembled a mild seizure.

Bella flopped onto her side with a theatrical sigh.

Thirteen minutes. That's how long I'd been running. Including the wheezing, the sulking, and the existential crisis halfway past the dog poo bin.

I opened my phone and logged it:

RUN ONE – THOUGHTS WHILE MOVING

Breathing resembles haunted kettle

Overtaken by toddler: psychological trauma

Park bench is my soulmate

Bella has emotionally checked out

Calves are blinking SOS

May be dying

A child nearby demanded a Calippo with the desperation of a man on death row. I'd never wanted an ice lolly more in my life. Or a defibrillator.

We limped back home. Bella leading, me trailing like a man dragging invisible anvils. I shuffled up the driveway like I'd just returned from war.

The front door was locked. Of course it was. Bella barked once—"your problem"—and disappeared round the back.

Eventually, I fumbled the keys and collapsed into the kitchen. The air was warm. The smell was pasta. The laughter was Connie.

She was seated, mug in hand, looking like serenity incarnate.

"How was your run?" she asked.

I didn't speak. I just lay on the floor and made a sound somewhere between a groan and a mating call for distressed walruses.

She sipped. "So... when's the BBC documentary filming?"

"I think I pulled something."

"Hopefully not a muscle. You might need one later."

I propped myself up just enough to open the laptop.

TRAINING LOG: WEEK ONE Run One: Duration – 13 minutes Distance – 1.2 miles (possibly exaggerated) Obstacles: pride, gravity, toddler

Triumphs:

Lived

Setbacks:

Everything else

Notes:

Reconsider sport

Reconsider adulthood

Purchase ice packs

Quavers kid has superior VO2 max

Do not Google "heart murmurs" after beer

Bella dropped a tennis ball on my face. Connie kissed the top of my head and said, "Only another hundred-something miles to go."

She left the room. I groaned. Or laughed. It was hard to tell.

Run one was done. Run one was technically complete.

Chapter 6: The Garage of Judgement

I arrived at the grease-streaked gates of Simmons & Sons Motor Repairs at exactly 7:58 a.m.—which, in the ancient rituals of the workshop, was considered "heroically on time." The car, my beloved 2003 Ford Focus Estate (currently held together by rust, pigeon droppings, and unresolved trauma), coughed itself to a stop like a consumptive badger and rolled into its usual parking spot—wedged tightly between a Volvo that had last moved during the Bush administration, and something that may once have been a Ford Fiesta but now looked more like a moss-covered relic from a failed time-travel experiment.

Inside the car, I sat staring at my passenger seat with the same dread one might reserve for an unexploded bomb or a relative holding a Tupperware of 'experimental' lasagne. There it lay. The Bag.

A gym bag. Black. Nylon. Slightly deformed, like it had been kicked repeatedly by fate. I'd packed it the night before, in what I now recognised as a moment of deranged optimism after watching a motivational video narrated by a man who sounded like he ironed his abs daily and urinated electrolyte water.

The contents were as follows:

A pair of trainers with soles worn so thin they offered the same cushioning as a wet envelope.

A high-vis vest the colour of irradiated custard, so bright it could be seen from the ISS.

An energy gel packet that had expired during the Obama presidency and was now inflating like it had opinions.

I opened the door, and the cold morning air hit me like a slap from an offended Victorian aunt. I stepped out, dressed for work but burdened with the emotional weight of a man who had Googled "beginner triathlon death rate" the night before and was unsatisfied with the answer.

Dan was already there, naturally—leaning against the roller shutter with a mug of coffee and an expression like he'd just caught me urinating in the holy font.

"Morning," he muttered, with the same tone you'd use to greet a man who'd just confessed to owning a ventriloquist dummy.

He looked at the gym bag.

"What's that?"

"My kit."

His eyebrows rose slowly. "For what?"

"I might go for a run later," I said, attempting nonchalance. What I achieved was somewhere between mild stroke and confused flamingo.

Dan stared. Then laughed. Not just a chuckle. A full, wheezing, knee-slapping guffaw that echoed around the yard and startled a seagull into flight.

"Oh, you're serious," he said, wiping a tear. "You poor, dumb bastard."

I ignored him. Just. And made for the side entrance, my gym bag thumping against my hip like a metronome of poor decision-making.

Inside, the familiar scent of hot oil, old socks, and burnt toast wrapped around me like a greasy duvet. Kerry was already at the reception desk, a beacon of sarcasm wrapped in leopard print and eyeliner, typing with one hand while annihilating a bacon bap with the other.

She glanced up, peered at the bag, and smirked.

"Morning, Ironman."

I stopped dead. "Who told you?"

"Dan did," she said, gesturing toward the door like she'd just expelled a fart and was proud of it. "Said you're training for one of those masochism tri-things. Swim, bike, collapse."

"It's just a hobby," I muttered, placing the bag down as gently as if it contained shame—which, in many ways, it did.

Kerry snorted. "So was gambling for my ex-husband. Now he lives in a caravan and owes money to a man named 'Clive the Nose'."

Dan wandered in, still grinning. "So, what stage are you at? Buying things you don't understand or diagnosing yourself with obscure ailments?"

"A little of both," I said. "Last night I spent forty minutes reading about plantar fasciitis."

Jim, our senior mechanic and local prophet of doom, emerged from beneath a van. He was wiping his hands on a rag that looked like it had fought in the trenches.

"Plantar what?"

"Foot pain," I said.

Jim nodded sagely. "That's what you get for running without cause. Evolution gave us legs for escaping bears and pub fights. Anything else is vanity."

Kerry raised her mug. "Hear, hear."

I attempted to focus on my job card—brake pads, oil change, minor service—but every ten minutes someone would pop their head in, say "Ironman" in a tone of amused disbelief, and walk off laughing.

By 10:00 a.m., even the Snap-on rep, Pete, had heard. He leaned against a tool cabinet and grinned like a man who'd just seen someone eat a wasp.

"You doing a triathlon?" he said. "Bloody hell. I once got a stitch watching the London Marathon on telly."

"Training's going well," I said.

"Yeah? You look like you train by sprinting to the fridge."

***

37

And then came lunchtime.

At precisely 12:03 p.m., I stood outside the changing cupboard cradling my kit bag like a war widow holding her late husband's pipe. The mood was tense. The lighting, fluorescent and unforgiving. I could feel my heart beating—not from anticipation or athletic readiness, but from the sheer anxiety of stepping into public view in clothing designed for people with sinew, not sandwiches.

I changed in silence.

The fluorescent yellow vest went on first. It clung to my torso like a skin graft made from highlighters. Next, the compression shorts, which had been advertised as "sculpting" but seemed more interested in "suffocating." They provided no support— emotional or otherwise—and created an alarming silhouette that could best be described as a baby seal in a bin bag.

Finally, the shoes—cracking slightly at the seams, as if protesting their sudden reactivation after a peaceful life in the wardrobe.

I emerged.

And everything... stopped.

Dan, Jason, Jim, and Kerry were mid-conversation when they turned and laid eyes upon me. The silence was so sudden it could have been bottled and sold as social anxiety concentrate.

Dan was the first to speak. "Dear God," he breathed, almost reverently. "You've done it. You've found the outfit that makes both yellow and spandex worse."

Jason dropped a pork pie. "You look like a condom someone left in the sun."

Jim squinted. "Nope. Not a condom. One of them novelty balloons. You know, the ones they twist into sad animals at children's parties. Except you're the before photo."

Kerry tilted her head. "Is that... is that your real body? Or are you smuggling a laundry basket?"

I opened my mouth to defend myself but immediately realised there was no good way to say, "This outfit is moisture-wicking" when your nipples are clearly losing a fight with the fabric.

"You've got the energy of a nervous meerkat at a fireworks display." said Dan. "Are you sure you're going for a run and not auditioning for a children's safety video?"

I took a deep breath. A bad idea. The vest sucked into every contour of my shame like clingfilm over chicken soup.

"I thought I'd do a short loop," I managed.

Jim raised an eyebrow. "A loop round what? The car park? Because if I were you, I wouldn't go further than thirty feet dressed like a radioactive traffic cone with body image issues."

"Don't forget the shoes," added Kerry. "They scream 'built for comfort, abandoned by performance.'"

A customer—middle-aged, tattooed, clearly delighted to have walked in mid-roast—paused by the counter and gestured toward me.

"My goodness, I didn't know the circus was hiring again."

Another customer, barely suppressing laughter, joined in. "Is this for a bet?"

"No," I said.

"Well," he grinned, "you should've made it one. You'd have at least walked away with something other than trauma."

"Lads," said Dan, wiping tears from his eyes, "I can't let him go outside like this. The council will issue a warning. Planes might try to land on him."

Jim nodded gravely. "Also, there are children out there. Think of the children."

I looked down at myself. At the vest. At the shorts. At the feet that had not moved from the changing room door. My knees suddenly locked up in protest, my legs forming a soft coup.

"I—maybe I'll... go after work," I muttered.

"Good idea," said Dan. "That way it'll be dark. Fewer witnesses."

Jason, barely holding it together, added, "Wear a trench coat. Or a poncho. Or better yet—a different identity."

Even Kerry looked vaguely sympathetic. "You'll get there, Ian. Not in that outfit. Or with that body. But spiritually."

I backed into the changing cupboard like a burglar who'd entered the wrong house and been greeted by a support group for sarcasm.

Back in my work clothes, I re-emerged to muted chuckles and a polite round of applause from a passing delivery driver.

"To be fair," said Dan, "you lasted longer than expected. Mentally, anyway. Physically you didn't even reach the threshold."

"Brave attempt," Kerry added. "If you'd made it outside, we were planning to record your sprint from the embarrassment. I'd already started a TikTok account: @NeonNightmare."

Jim tossed me a biscuit. "Here. Carb-load emotionally."

I took the biscuit, sat down at my workstation, and sighed.

Somewhere in my phone was a training plan. A noble, structured, well-intentioned set of goals. One of those goals had been "run at lunchtime." Instead, I'd managed "get dressed, be emotionally demolished, eat biscuit."

Was it progress? Debatable. But it was something.

As the afternoon wore on, the memory of my attempted transformation lingered like a fart in a lift. Every so often, someone would pause, glance at me, and giggle.

Kerry printed a new sign for the staffroom:

"MOTs From £49.95 — Lycra-Based Delusions Free With Every Oil Change"

By the time five o'clock rolled around, I wasn't even faking productivity. I stuffed my kit into my bag with the desperate energy of a man trying to bury evidence. Just as I made it to the door, Dan looked up from his desk and called out:

"You off for that run, then? Or just fleeing the scene?"

"No."

"Shame," said Jim. "We'd warmed up the defibrillator."

I climbed into my car, took a deep breath, and glanced at the mirror. The face that stared back looked tired, mocked, and vaguely radioactive. But beneath the bruised ego was the stubborn flicker of someone who still hadn't quit.

So maybe I didn't run today. But I'd gotten one step closer.

And honestly, some days, putting on the vest is its own kind of victory.

Even if everyone else thinks you look like an overinflated banana who lost a bet.

Chapter 7: Turbo in the Kitchen

There exists a particular breed of hope so rare, so catastrophically misguided, that scientists have yet to officially catalogue it — the kind that bursts into life mere moments before a piece of fitness equipment arrives. Not the noble, character-building variety that fuels tales of transformation. No, I mean the delusional kind, the sort of frenzied optimism that convinces you that merely purchasing an object will somehow download an entire lifestyle directly into your personality. It's the same illogical optimism that convinces a man that if he buys a guitar, he will, within a week, be smashing out stadium tours or that buying a set of chef's knives will somehow turn him into Gordon Ramsay, despite still burning toast on setting one.

It wasn't, regrettably, my first entanglement with this species of lunacy. My garage was already home to a carefully curated gallery of failed fitness romances: a yoga mat so permanently curled at the edges it resembled a taxidermied armadillo; resistance bands so intricately tangled they could be repurposed as a warning to future civilisations; and a pull-up bar that, during its brief and ill-advised residency in the doorway, tore a fist-sized hole in the plaster, damaging my ego far more than my shoulder.

The kettlebell phase had ended on the day one of the wretched things met the bones of my bare foot, prompting me to emit a sound so unnatural and primal that the dog, Bella, still refuses to look me in the eye. We don't talk about the barefoot running phase at all — chiefly because it concluded in a bog, cost me two toenails, and left me walking for a week like a constipated crab trying to cross a gravel driveway.

And yet, this time felt different. This time there were wheels involved.

It began, as so many mistakes do, with a late-night internet search: "Beginner indoor bike trainer (cheap but effective but mostly cheap)". Within minutes, I was knee-deep in gear reviews, performance charts, and sweaty men on YouTube whisper-yelling about cadence ratios into GoPro's strapped to their own faces, all with the zeal of people who have not experienced joy in years.

My browser history quickly began to resemble the research file of a man planning an unsanctioned escape across Europe by bicycle. Words like "fluid resistance" and "flywheel inertia" were tossed at me with the casual cruelty of someone assuming I had even the faintest grasp of physics. One model boasted "progressive resistance curves based on fluid dynamics," which I assumed was either a technical marvel or an alarming euphemism. Another offered "dual-flywheel smart responsiveness," which sounded like a medical condition or the sort of feature that required regular firmware updates and the alignment of several moons.

Both looked expensive. Then, through the haze of marketing jargon, I spotted it — the perfect middle ground. Not so cheap it would explode upon contact with air, and not so advanced that it would demand my Wi-Fi password every Sunday evening. It was even on sale — slightly — if you squinted, factored in a healthy dose of denial, and ignored the "original price" they'd almost certainly invented that morning. I clicked Buy Now with the urgency of a man deleting an incriminating browser tab.

The box arrived on Tuesday. It was enormous, obnoxiously so — the sort of box that silently informs your neighbours you are either overcompensating or have bought something inflatable that will get you blacklisted from the local residents' association. I intercepted the delivery like a man smuggling contraband, timing my manoeuvre so Connie was still outside in the garden. Bella barked once; I lobbed her a biscuit and whispered "loyalty" like a mafia boss bribing a witness. The sheer bulk of the box blotted out the kitchen window light as I wrestled it through the front door. The kitchen was the only place with enough space, so I wedged it between the fridge and the back door, where it stood looming like an unfamiliar relative who's come to stay indefinitely.

Inside, the box contained a collection of metal parts, one mysterious plastic artefact and a multilingual instruction manual that appeared to have been written by a malfunctioning robot on the verge of a nervous breakdown — in every language except English. I stashed the receipt somewhere truly unfindable (admitting defeat later is always easier if you destroy the evidence first) and began my construction project.

Assembly tested not only my patience but also my engineering skill and my capacity for remaining polite to inanimate objects. Thirty-seven YouTube tutorials later, I had a partially assembled trainer, one bleeding thumb, and a dog chewing on the manual like it was a sworn enemy. I can rebuild a clutch blindfolded, but I could not, for the life of me, work out how to tighten the saddle without risking accidental castration. One bolt was labelled "secure gently," which is not a phrase any self-respecting mechanic has ever respected. Either it's tight, or it's loose. "Gently" is what you do with a sleeping baby, not with hardware that will later support the weight of a man flailing in Lycra.

I phoned Dan to help me interpret one particularly vague diagram. "Is that a medieval torture rack?" he asked. "Not intentionally," I replied. He hung up without saying goodbye. Eventually, the whole contraption stood upright — or at least stable enough not to collapse unless aggressively breathed on. All that was missing was the bike.

The bike "lived" — a generous term — in the shed. The shed door stuck as though it had been welded shut by the sheer weight of years worth of broken promises. When it finally gave way, I nearly toppled backwards into the compost heap. Inside was a museum of unwanted things: broken tools, deflated footballs, a garden chair that now served as luxury accommodation for wasps. The air smelled like Bella had contributed to the atmosphere. Somewhere in this archaeological site was my bike — a relic from an earlier, more optimistic version of me who had once cycled to work for two whole consecutive weeks. I spotted it by the edge of a tyre protruding from under a mouldy tarp and a tangled hose. Pulling it free felt like disturbing an ancient burial ground. The frame was lacquered with grime, the chain rusted into a modernist sculpture, and a spider the size of a crumpet had declared squatters rights.

Dragging it inside was a cardio workout in itself, akin to wrestling Jack into his swimming kit — awkward, noisy, and liable to leave lasting trauma on both sides. It clipped door frames, scraped tiles, and left behind a brown trail of mysterious filth. I parked it next to the trainer like a teacher introducing two pupils they just know are going to hate each other.

I didn't ride that night. No, one must prepare oneself mentally for such an endeavour. Emotional preparation is the athlete's secret weapon. In this case, it meant staring at the thing while consuming biscuits straight from the packet and reassuring myself that Geraint Thomas probably did the same. The following morning, I dressed for war: compression shorts last worn in 2019 and smelling like the year itself, a hoodie designed for warming up but doubling as a portable sauna. I clipped my phone into the handlebar mount and launched the app. "Welcome to Spin & Grin: Endurance Foundations!" chirped a voice far too chipper for that time of day.

Mounting the bike was an athletic spectacle in itself. I approached it like a man trying to mount a mildly annoyed Shetland pony — cautiously, with one eye on the possible escape routes. I threw a leg over, missed the saddle by several inches, and found myself suspended in a mid-air squat, wobbling like a flamingo in a hurricane. Bella appeared in the doorway, her ears twitching in the universal canine sign for "I regret being domesticated." My foot searched for the pedal with all the accuracy of a man attempting to plug in a USB stick blindfolded. The clip refused to engage. Press, twist, press again — nothing. Eventually, more by accident than skill, one foot was clipped in, the other dangled uselessly, and my centre of gravity hovered somewhere over Belgium.

I began pedalling, knees pumping like a wind-up toy. The flywheel engaged with a low hum, somewhere between "approaching lawnmower" and "desk fan from hell." Bella stared at me as if she had just witnessed a crime. At the first sprint interval, she barked once, then vacated the room entirely, presumably to escape the imminent explosion. The turbo rattled like a Peugeot missing a cylinder. I adjusted a tension knob with the pointless optimism of a man tuning a carburettor on a toaster. Three minutes in, I was wheezing. Seven minutes in, a rogue spoon fell from the counter and I screamed as though the turbo had burst into flames. Ten minutes in, one child wandered in mid-rant about something involving Minecraft and the laws of armed conflict. Ellie followed, cereal bowl in hand, eyebrows raised to an altitude that required oxygen. "You know we can all hear you breathing like that?" she said. "It's like Darth Vader got stuck in a spin class." She rolled her eyes. "If my friends knew this was happening in our kitchen, I'd have to change schools."

Then Spotify decided to play the Peppa Pig Greatest Hits. I sprinted — to the Bing Bong Song. Something in my soul detached and drifted into the next county. When I unclipped, my legs gave way with the theatrics of a Victorian heroine swooning at bad news. I collapsed onto the tiles like a sack of condemned potatoes. The hoodie clung to me as if trying to escape with me inside it. The floor glistened with sweat. Bella sniffed me from a safe distance, trying to determine if this was a medical emergency or just another Tuesday.

***

Later, when I regained enough motor function to operate a phone, I attempted a triumphant selfie. I framed it carefully: red face, heroic tilt, just enough sweat to imply effort without causing alarm. What I didn't notice was the collapsed hoodie draped over a chair, Bella's rope toy lodged in the fruit bowl, and my water bottle on its side, leaking onto a roll of kitchen towel. The comments were instant and merciless: "Why does your kitchen look like it just ran a marathon?" "Is that your dog judging you in the background?" "You look like you've been rescued from a well." "Blink twice if you're okay." "Respect for the effort, but your fruit bowl needs therapy." I deleted it after seven minutes. But I kept the photo. For the record.

***

At 3 a.m., my calves cramped like they were auditioning for Riverdance. I woke whimpering, attempted a stretch, and accidentally kicked Connie in the shin. She muttered something ancient and profane and rolled away for good. The children, over breakfast, behaved as though nothing had happened, which somehow made it worse. They exchanged glances over cereal boxes like junior scientists observing a doomed experiment. Ellie whispered, "He's definitely going to do it again," and Jack nodded gravely.

***

By week two, Bella had developed a strategy. During a climbing interval — thighs trembling, lungs issuing plumbing noises — she dropped her rope toy directly behind the rear wheel. One bark. I ignored her. She nudged it closer. The rope snagged somewhere unspeakable. There was a thunk, a wobble, a yelp (mine), and the whole contraption threatened to fold in on itself. Bella retreated to the hallway, eyes narrowed, rope abandoned like evidence. The message was clear: "This is not who you used to be."

***

By the weekend, Connie had begun giving the turbo setup the same look she reserved for Jack's PE kit after a muddy rugby match. I decided to clean it. In the process, I knocked it over, cracked my shin on the pedal, spilled energy drink into the toaster socket, and created a smell so potent that Bella fled the room at speed. The entire kitchen smelled like a chemistry experiment that had lost faith. While dragging the bin out front, I ran into Steve from next door — the kind of man who owns three kinds of gloves and says things like "good composting weather." He tilted his head. "Heard a strange noise yesterday," he said. "Like someone using a vacuum while crying?" I nodded. "That's me. That's my soul on a bike." He handed me a flyer for a yoga class. I think it was a hint.

That night, Connie caught me staring at the turbo. She asked, "What are you actually trying to prove with this?" I could have said fitness. Health. Midlife reinvention. But instead I said, "That I'm still allowed to change." She looked at me for a long time, then said, "Then keep going."

And so I do. And now, with three weeks of indoor cycling under my increasingly strained belt, I stand here in my kitchen — sweat-drenched, oxygen-deprived, and yet unbowed — to deliver my victory speech. Ladies, gentlemen, and concerned domestic pets, today we mark a new chapter in the annals of human endurance. Not since the great explorers charted unknown continents has a man achieved so much while moving so little. I have conquered the brutal terrain between the fridge and the recycling bin. I have endured the searing climbs of simulated hills while navigating the treacherous crosswinds of an oscillating desk fan that smells faintly of loft dust. I have powered through the psychological warfare of the Peppa Pig soundtrack and emerged not merely alive, but triumphant. My resting heart rate remains "slightly startled," my average speed would still lose to an arthritic swan, and my dog's respect is in free fall — but my resolve is granite. This turbo trainer is no longer just a piece of equipment; it is my Everest, my Colosseum, my stage at Wembley. And when history judges me — as surely it must — let the record show that I did not quit, I did not falter, and I most certainly did not let the Bing Bong Song break me. In the grand tradition of all great champions, I dedicate this victory to my loyal supporters: my long-suffering family, my deeply judgmental dog, and the brave spoon that fell from the counter that first day and took the noise for the team. The world may not yet be ready for the full force of what I have become — but mark my words: this is only the beginning.

Interlude: The WhatsApp Manifesto

A grilling of Ian. Court is now in session.

Dan: Right, agenda item one — Exhibit A: "I clicked Register whilst holding bin liners." Plea?
Me: Guilty. With mitigating biscuits.
Kev: I move to establish a baseline of stupidity. On a scale from "air fryer burns" to "DIY vasectomy," where are we?
Baz: He's entered IRONMAN Wales, Kev. We're beyond scales. We're into folklore.

Dan: Mr Dawson, please explain your training so far.
Me: I've built a comprehensive spreadsheet. Tabs. Formulas. Colour coding.
Baz: And legs? Any progress on those?
Me: Pending delivery.

Kev: Nutrition strategy?
Me: Biscuits. Aspirationally, rice.
Dan: Hydration?
Me: Tea.
Dan: Electrolytes?
Me: Salty crisps?
Baz: Not wrong, just... culinary.

Dan: Swimming ability?
Me: Think "elegant drowning."
Kev: Bike?
Me: Functions as a garden sculpture with pedals.
Baz: Run?
Me: More of a forward-leaning shuffle with optimistic branding.

Dan: Motivation, then. Why do this?
Me: To see if there's still a bit of me that isn't rust.
(Silence. Even WhatsApp types slower.)
Kev: Alright, that's disgustingly sincere. I hated it. Carry on.

Baz: Conditions of our support:

You will not die.

You will not make us run.

You will accept heckling as essential electrolytes.

Dan: Proposed team roles:
Me: Director of Reality Checks.
Kev: Head of Snacks & Unhelpful Facts.
Baz: Noise.
Sandra: Compliance & Darts-related sanctions.

Kev: Final question. On race day, if you cry on the run, will it be:
A) Scenic crying,
B) Angry crying, or
C) Welsh weather entering via your face?
Me: D) All of the above, with cola.

Baz: Verdict: permitted to proceed under supervision.
Dan: Case adjourned.
Kev: Pub?
Me: Recovery pub. With carbohydrates.
All: Aye.

Chapter 8: Lycra Crimes

Buying a tri-suit is not a rational act. It's a declaration of temporary insanity, an embroidered flag hoisted high over the crumbling fortress of one's self-respect. It is a stretchy, zippered leap of faith — like buying a cape because you once climbed a stepladder without falling off and fancied yourself as a superhero, albeit one with lower back pain and a beer gut. I stared at it in my online checkout basket for three days, circling it like a cat circling a hedgehog, knowing full well it would hurt but feeling somehow compelled to make contact. I read every review with forensic suspicion, compared sizes with the solemnity of a coroner noting cause of death, and zoomed in on every awkward product photo of anonymous men shaped like coat hangers who had clearly been blackmailed into modelling. None of them looked happy. One looked like he'd been vacuum-packed and was waiting for a rescue helicopter. Another looked like a freshly varnished corpse.

Eventually, I caved. Clicked Buy Now with the confidence of a man deliberately ignoring every flashing hazard light on the dashboard of his life. Because somewhere in the dark corridors of my brain, a tiny traitorous voice had whispered: "If you're going to make a complete fool of yourself, at least dress like it's deliberate." This is the exact kind of thinking that leads people to buy hoverboards, trampolines, and timeshares in Málaga.

***

It arrived mid-week in a matte black box with minimalist branding, the kind of packaging that sneers at you as you pick it up, muttering, "You? Really?" in Helvetica. The lettering declared "Performance Engineered." The box itself whispered, "You are not worthy." I carried it into the house like it might explode, or worse, be intercepted by Connie.

"More gear?" she asked without even looking up, the way a magistrate might say "Another parking violation?" to a repeat offender.

"It's... necessary," I said, trying for authority and managing only guilt.

"For what? Starting a crime-fighting syndicate?"

"For... airflow. And freedom of movement."

She raised one eyebrow without lifting her gaze from the laptop.

"You bought a Lycra onesie for airflow?"

"Tri-suit," I muttered, as if the technical term would transform the situation into something noble. "Technical fabric."

"Right. Good luck with that."

I waited until the house was empty to try it on. Even Bella left the room the moment I unzipped the packaging. She gave it one sniff, then backed away like it had mentioned the word "bath." Getting into it was a sport in itself. I managed to get one leg halfway in before realising I'd twisted it backwards. It took another five minutes to discover where my arms were meant to go, and by the time I'd inched it past my knees, I was sweating like a politician on a lie detector.

This morning, I stood in the kitchen with one arm still trapped inside the suit, trying not to pull a hamstring, and asked myself for the fifth time why I was doing this. Bella sat nearby, head tilted, wearing the same expression she reserves for watching me assemble flat-pack furniture: pity, confusion, and the faintest hint of contempt.

The first attempt was a full-blown farce. I got both legs in and one arm out before realising something had gone spectacularly wrong. I stared at my reflection — twisted like a pretzel and briefly wondered if I had accidentally purchased a Lycra straightjacket. I couldn't locate the neck hole. My elbow was approximately where my shoulder should be. For one surreal moment, I wondered if this was genuine sportswear or an elaborate sting operation designed to identify morons. Somewhere behind me, Bella sighed so heavily I considered apologising.

I finally figured it out, turned it around, and tried again, slower this time, like a man defusing a bomb with mittens on. By the time it was fully on I looked like a condom full of poorly managed expectations. The fabric was shinier than a nightclub floor and clung to me with the desperate intimacy of a tax inspector. Regions of my anatomy I'd spent decades politely ignoring were now being presented to the world in ultra-high definition. The zip climbed my back like it was trying to escape me.

I turned to the mirror. This wasn't sportswear. This was revenge clothing. I looked like a ham auditioning for a Marvel film. And yet... I couldn't stop staring.

I grabbed my bike, checked the tyres with the faux authority of a man who doesn't know what PSI means, then realised I'd left my water bottle in the fridge. I shuffled back inside, clopping in cleats like a malfunctioning tap dancer. As I bent to grab it, the tri-suit made a sound like someone opening a crisp packet during a funeral. Then it was time to leave. Too late to back out. I waited by the door like a burglar, praying no one saw me leave.

It was Dan's idea to do a group ride. "Bit of a test run," he said. "Get used to the kit. Build confidence." Translation: "Let's see how much public humiliation a grown man can absorb before needing counselling." Dan had done a few sportives and once signed up for a charity ride across Wales — although he bailed after Day Two, citing "knees, weather, and a haunted B&B." Still, he owned clipless pedals and had opinions about tyre pressure, which made him an expert by default.

***

We met just after 9 a.m., that smugly respectable time of day which says "serious" without tipping into "elite." I arrived early to adjust, warm up, and, if necessary, flee without witnesses. Dan rolled up dressed like a catalogue model for "Middle-Aged Adventure." Wraparound sunglasses. Fingerless gloves. A jersey with more zips than a psychopath's duffel bag. He looked almost competent.

"You look like you mean business," I said.
"I look like I'm avoiding responsibility," he replied. "Which, to be fair, I am. Figured a ride with you was marginally better than

defrosting the freezer or helping with phonics homework." He gave me a slow up-and-down. "And you look like a midlife crisis wrapped in clingfilm. So, we're off to a strong start."

I glanced down at the tri-suit — still clinging with the tenacity of an unwanted suitor. "It's supposed to be aerodynamic."
Dan snorted. "Mate, unless you're cycling through a wind tunnel at 60mph, the only thing you're streamlining is your dignity."

We were about to set off when Kev and Baz turned up. Kev wore what could only be described as a jacket last seen at a car boot sale in 1998 and carried a bottle of Lucozade like a lifeline. Baz emerged from his van holding a pastry and coffee, dressed for brunch, not battle.

"You're not riding?" I asked.
Kev laughed. "Mate, I'm here for moral support, not therapy."
Baz shook his head. "Lycra's a conspiracy. I'm just here to witness the implosion."

Dan checked his watch. "We doing this?" Apparently, we were.

We rolled down the road, Kev shouting, "Try not to humiliate yourselves before the first left turn!" Baz cupped his hands. "Text me when the paramedics need coordinates!" Kev added, "If something starts rattling — it's your self-esteem!" Baz: "STAY HYDRATED. TEARS AREN'T ELECTROLYTES!"

Dan didn't look back. "Ignore them," he muttered. "They're just jealous."
I nodded. "Of our decision-making skills? Or the chafing?" He didn't answer. Probably both.

Five minutes in, I couldn't feel my toes. Probably normal. Probably the "aerodynamic" effect: less blood, more speed. What am I doing? What if someone from work sees me? What if Simon drives past with a client and I end up as a cautionary tale? Dan called something back — I nodded, not having heard it, because my brain was busy deciding whether my shorts were cutting off circulation or my soul was quietly leaving my body.

We passed a man walking a ferret on a lead. Not hallucinating. Just Wales. Every bump in the road sent a blunt telegram to my spine. Every breeze reminded me exactly how "compressive" the tri-suit was. Taking it off now would be like peeling clingfilm off a hot chicken: undignified, messy, and likely to ruin someone's lunch.

The seat had the give of a brick wrapped in sandpaper. At work, things make sense: torque wrench, manual, predictable result. You don't tighten a bolt and hope it improves your character. This was sweaty, saddle-sore guesswork.

We took the long loop past Griffin Park. One hill near Victoria Avenue looked innocent until halfway up, where it presented the bill for every biscuit, pasty, and kebab of your adult life. A woman pushing a double buggy overtook us without breaking stride. Dan muttered, "She's probably on her fourth lap," while I concentrated on not decorating the pavement with my breakfast.

By Porthcawl Cricket Club, I'd sweated through most of the suit. The "performance-grade" padding had migrated somewhere near my kidneys. I tried to adjust mid-pedal, veered into Dan like a shopping trolley with a bent wheel. "Oi!" he shouted. "Save that move for the finish line, Wiggins."
"It's the padding," I hissed. "It's gone rogue."
Dan laughed. "You look like you're smuggling a beach towel through customs."

We stopped near the bowling green. I unclipped and attempted to dismount, but my legs staged an immediate walkout. I half-collapsed onto a bench. Tried to stand. My legs politely declined further participation. I hovered mid-rise, knees wobbling like a baby deer on a frozen trampoline, before surrendering back into the seat.

"I don't think I'm built for this," I admitted.
"Engine's fine," Dan said, handing me a flapjack. "Just looks like someone wrapped a perfectly good motor in the bodywork of a scrap Punto."

We sat there, two grown men dressed for a race that wasn't happening, pretending not to notice how long it was taking our heart rates to return to human levels. A plastic cup tumbled past in the breeze. Somewhere a toddler screamed at a pigeon. It felt thematically perfect.

"Why'd you sign up for the IRONMAN thing?" Dan asked eventually.
I hesitated. Not because I didn't know, but because saying it out loud again felt like it would make it dangerously real. No grand epiphany. Just wear and tear. Something inside rattling loose until I couldn't ignore it anymore.
"Dunno. Needed something. Something that didn't involve bin bags or brake fluid."
Dan nodded. "Fair enough. Also a great excuse to buy gear you don't understand."
"Exactly."

We clipped back in and rode on. Slower. In sync. No records broken. No applause. But it was progress. We showed up. In Lycra. On purpose. And, absurdly, that counted.

***

Back home, I peeled the tri-suit off in stages, like wallpaper from a condemned building. The zip had fused with my skin. Out of the shower, I felt like someone had tried to tenderise me for stew. Every muscle ached — even ones I was fairly sure belonged to someone else. I dried with a hand towel from the radiator, covering roughly 12% of my surface area, then limped downstairs like I was auditioning for the "before" shot in a physiotherapy advert. Halfway down, something twitched in my calf and I made a sound not recognised by any human language.

I eased into the armchair like a king returning from war.
"You were gone for 90 minutes," Connie said.
"In that time, I saw God, hit a pothole, and questioned every life decision I've ever made."
"So, a normal day?"

I closed my eyes. The sofa groaned in sympathy. Somewhere upstairs, a child shouted about Wi-Fi. My legs twitched in Morse code for help.

"Now I've sat down, I may never get up again."
"Brilliant. I'll fetch you a bell."

Silence settled over the room, broken only by the tick of the clock and the slow, deliberate crunch of her biscuit — savoured like victory. Even time seemed to hesitate. I wondered if a man could get a quad cramp in his soul.
Without looking at me, Connie said, "You'll do it though, won't you? The IRONMAN thing."
"Probably."
"Even if it breaks you?"
"Especially if it does."
She smiled faintly. "Give me a heads-up next time you plan something completely unhinged."

She turned a page like delivering a final verdict. I leaned back, closed my eyes, and let the sofa claim me. The madness had begun. And I had witnesses.

Chapter 9: Resistance is Utterly Futile

It wasn't that I wanted to start strength training. It's just that every other post in the triathlon forum said I had to, and apparently, I'm easily bullied by men with delts the size of livestock.

I was three biscuits deep into a packet of chocolate Hobnobs, casually googling "triathlon strength training plan for beginners who hate pain and have low moral fibre," when I stumbled across a forum titled:
"Lifting for Triathletes Who Cry Easily."

Finally, I thought. My people.

Ten minutes later, I was waist-deep in advice from men named Troy and Brant who looked like they'd been bench-pressing resentment since birth. Every post read like a sermon at the Church of Perpetual Protein.

"Deadlifts are life. Train your posterior chain or prepare for shame."
"No pain, no gains. No glutes, no glory."
"Your hamstrings are your powerplants. Fuel them, brother."

They spoke in inspirational quotes and light steroid fumes.

"Core stability is crucial," they chirped.
"Leg strength means run strength," they insisted.
"Don't be that guy who skips gym work and ends up pulling a hamstring tying his laces."

I didn't know who that guy was, but I had a strong suspicion his name was Ian.

In a fit of optimism, I searched for something gentler —
"strength for dads who have accepted mortality." I found a bloke from Surrey called Craig, who promised "zero-intensity workouts for reluctant athletes." That felt achievable. Until I realised Craig was filming from a beach in Bali, topless, glowing with smug abs and the sort of tan that screams "tax exile."

One minute he was explaining single-leg balance drills, the next I was watching a squirrel steal a Kit Kat from a builder's lunchbox. Classic YouTube spiral. Sixty minutes later, I had learned nothing but had subscribed to a channel called Core Mayhem for Legends.

Naturally, before lifting anything, I did what every triathlete does when overwhelmed by fear and inadequacy — I bought equipment.

I ordered a "Home Strength Kit – Starter Plus" online, which promised big results in a small footprint — much like Bella, if Bella were made of rubber and self-belief she couldn't back up.

Then, in a fit of madness, I ordered a "Complete Resistance Training Bundle" from a website that also sold novelty egg poachers and tactical flashlights. The checkout offered an add-on: tactical gloves. I had no idea what that meant, but assumed if I wore them, strength would transfer by osmosis.

I shut the laptop, crumbs cascading down my chest, and felt the familiar dread of a man about to make his garage smell worse.

Thus began my journey into strength training — from the comfort of my sofa, fortified by biscuits and delusion.

With the misplaced confidence of a man who once bought a neck massager that became a doorstop, I declared the garage my personal gym. I downloaded a "garage-friendly" plan containing words like "mobility," "activation," and "deadlift" — all of which sounded like stages of possession. The warm-up alone was two pages long. By the end of it, I needed a nap.

Two days later, a suspiciously cheerful box arrived, labelled "Home Strength Kit – Elite Bundle," as though it might contain hope. The cover featured a man mid-squat, his back muscles so defined they could be used for orienteering.

Inside I found:

Resistance bands so tight they could restrain aircraft.

A kettlebell made of "poly-iron," which I assumed meant plastic with confidence issues.

A pair of push-up bars that looked better suited as coat hooks.

And the legendary tactical gloves, which made me feel like Jason Bourne if he'd been sponsored by Poundland.

A leaflet screamed Get Shredded at Any Age! — which read less like encouragement and more like a threat.

I tried stretching the "extreme" band and managed only to look like I was fighting an invisible anaconda. It didn't move. I did. Tremblingly.

Still, I felt ready. Until I remembered the garage.

***

The garage, of course, was not ready for anything.

I opened the side door and was greeted by the unholy smell of stale oil, mouse history, and whatever nightmare lived inside the cooler box. The light bulb flickered weakly, like it too had lost hope. Beneath car magazines from 2004 and what might once have been a pigeon, I found my dumbbells — rusted, taped together, and exuding a distinct aura of tetanus.

They made a sound when lifted — not a crisp metallic clang but a thunk-squeak, like a pensioner exiting a beanbag.

I needed a mat, because all the videos featured attractive people on pristine mats, stretching like optimistic starfish. The only option was the old yoga mat under the turbo trainer, now fused to the floor by sweat.

Plan B: a doormat from the back wall, its faded WELCOME reduced to WE ME. Close enough.

I laid it out and attempted a push-up. My elbows immediately declared independence. The second attempt was a controlled collapse. The third was a nap.

The video cheerily suggested Romanian deadlifts. I looked like a flamingo auditioning for Swan Lake and missing every cue. One leg flailed, the other begged for death, and I nearly head-butted a paint tin.

The plank lasted ten seconds before everything south of my eyebrows gave up. Mountain climbers resembled polite knee lifts performed by a man trying not to wake the baby Jesus.

If anyone had walked in, I'd have said I was auditioning for Cirque du Tragic. Halfway through my humiliation, I flashed back to the last time I'd "lifted weights" — the gym induction of 2011.

Back then, I'd fallen for a poster that said, "Free Induction: Find Your Power."

My power turned out to be fainting decoratively.

The trainer, Darren — forearms like Christmas hams, tattoo reading Pain Is Weakness Leaving the Biceps — introduced me to medieval machinery. The leg press folded me neatly in half. The rowing machine sighed audibly. I mistook the pec deck for a seat and sat there like I was waiting for the bus.

"Keep your core engaged," Darren grunted.
"My core left five minutes ago," I wheezed, sliding off a Swiss ball like melting cheese.

The treadmill launched me into orbit before I'd even located the stop button. I staggered out with a free protein bar and post-traumatic DOMS.

A week later the gym emailed: Your goals miss you. I marked it as spam.

Back in the garage, I was mid-squat with a paint tin of Storm Grey – Semi-Gloss when the door creaked open.

Connie appeared, holding a laundry basket, wearing the expression of a woman discovering her husband's new religion.

She surveyed the scene: rusted dumbbells, sweat, a doormat that said WE ME, and me trembling like a waiter with soup.

"IRONMAN training?"

"Functional conditioning," I gasped.

"Looks like strategic collapse." She nodded, turned to leave, and called over her shoulder, "Put your will somewhere visible, just in case."

***

The next morning, I woke sore in areas I didn't know had grievance procedures. My obliques, dormant since a violent sneeze in 2016, had staged an uprising. Even brushing my teeth felt like advanced Pilates.

At breakfast, I lowered myself into a chair like a nervous parachutist. Connie slid the cereal toward me as though feeding a wounded badger.

"Big session yesterday?"
I nodded. Mistake. Neck muscles revolted.
"Remember, no one's paying you for this."
"This is for growth," I croaked, giving her a weak thumbs-up.
"Is that what we're calling limping now?"

I ate in slow motion, chewing with the heroic determination of a man auditioning for a soup advert.

That afternoon, for reasons now classified as psychological self-harm, I attempted another session.

New video: Strength & Stability for Endurance Athletes – Beginner Friendly! The coach had a grin powered by kale and delusion.

"Just a light circuit," he said. "You should feel energised, not exhausted."

Lies.

Five minutes in, I'd lost feeling in my thumbs. Attempting a "reverse lunge to high knee with twist," I toppled sideways, grabbed the ride-on mower and ended up straddling it like a jousting knight who'd forgotten the horse part.

Connie appeared silently, filming.
"For Instagram?" I wheezed.
"For insurance."

Next came Superman raises. Apparently, one must lie flat and lift all limbs as if flying. I managed the lying part with distinction. My back creaked, my hamstrings made their objections clear, and the video instructor chirped, "Engage your core!"

My core had emigrated.

By Glute Bridges, I was hallucinating. The paint tin rolled away. My breathing resembled a dying airbed. I caught sight of myself reflected in the tumble dryer: a pink, quivering man mid-meltdown. So this, I thought, is what rock bottom wears.

The "cool-down" was mainly me pretending to stretch while questioning the structural integrity of my existence.

"Great job, athletes!" said the instructor. I considered phoning Trading Standards.

Bella wandered in, sighed with Shakespearean gravity, and left.

Eventually, I dragged myself upright using a rusted wrench, producing noises not found in nature.

By evening, I was moving like a cupboard full of cutlery. Sitting required logistics. Standing required prayer. I dropped a cushion and stared at it for a full minute before accepting it was gone forever.

Ellie walked in. "You alright?"
"Define 'alright.'"
"You're making grandad noises."
"I'm realigning my hips with destiny."

She retreated. Even the dog avoided eye contact.

The TV showed a triathlon documentary — some sculpted overachiever running uphill like gravity was just a suggestion. My phone buzzed.

Dan: "Still breathing?"
Me: "Barely. My glutes have unionised."
Dan: "Did the dumbbells win?"
Me: "They've claimed independence."
Dan: "Stretch. Then beer. Then more beer."

Stretching sounded ideal until my knee made the death-rattle of a fax machine.

Jack wandered in, brandishing the iPad. "Dad, look at this — a monkey falls off a scooter and screams like a goose."

We watched it twice. He laughed both times. I saw myself in that monkey.

"Dad?"
"Yeah?"
"Are you gonna win the IRONMAN?"
I looked at my trembling limbs. "I'm aiming to finish without medical attention."
"Cool," he said. "Can I have a biscuit?"

And that, really, summed it up.

If this IRONMAN dream was to continue, I'd need more than determination and a doormat that read WE ME. I'd need snacks, supervision, possibly a priest, and almost certainly a corporate partnership with Deep Heat.

Two days later — or possibly three; time had dissolved into muscle ache — I limped back into the garage, every bone groaning in anticipation. The dumbbells glared. The doormat whispered betrayal.

I took a breath, cracked most of my spine, and hit play.

Because resistance training, as it turns out, is utterly futile — but so am I.

Interlude: The Gear Spreadsheet

I simply wanted a list — a modest, sensible inventory of the few items I'd need to transform from sedentary grease-monkey into amphibious Lycra enthusiast. A wetsuit that didn't resemble a bin bag, a bicycle that didn't look stolen, and running shoes that wouldn't set my arches on fire.

But by the end of the evening, my innocent list had mutated into a twelve-tab, colour-coded abomination titled:
TRIATHLON KIT MASTER FILE — DO NOT DELETE (I'M SERIOUS, CONNIE).

It was less a spreadsheet and more a cry for help with formulas.

There was a tab for price comparisons, naturally — because why spend responsibly when you can spend scientifically? A tab for "Future Upgrades," which essentially functioned as a financial suicide note. And one titled "Misc," which contained all the mysterious artefacts I didn't understand but had convinced myself were vital to human survival: race belts, salt tablets, CO_2 canisters, and something called a saddle bottle cage which, judging by the photo, could probably power a moon base.

I also added a section titled "Potential Deal Breakers," where I logged anything that might one day end my triathlon career — chafing, bankruptcy, or the inevitable moment I realise no amount of carbon fibre will make me fast, aerodynamic, or interesting at dinner parties.

Then came my "Emergency Kit Reserves" tab — a euphemism for Things I Bought at 2:14 a.m. While Spiralling. It included: four pairs of socks marketed as performance-enhancing, two tubs of chamois cream (one "for sensitive areas," the other "for people who've given up"), and a pot of electrolyte tablets that smelled like a cross between bleach and fear.

Every item was cross-referenced with discount codes, user reviews, and my own increasingly unhinged colour-coding system:

Green: Essential (says YouTube).

Yellow: Possibly useful (if I ever leave the garage).

Orange: Questionable, but I was drunk.

Red: Financial self-harm.

At one point, I briefly considered adding a tab called "Mental Preparation." I stared at the empty cell for a full minute before realising that if I needed Excel to find emotional stability, the battle was already lost.

It was around this time Connie appeared, drawn by the faint smell of despair and new plastic. She leaned over my shoulder as I adjusted the axis on a graph labelled Projected Performance Gains vs Financial Ruin.

"Are you budgeting for a second bike?" she asked, incredulous.

"It's called contingency planning," I said.

"For what? A midlife Tour de France?"

"It's important to have options."

She made a sound somewhere between a sigh and a death rattle — the one she uses for moments of deep personal tragedy, like Bella eating her slippers or me saying "investment piece." Then she patted my shoulder like a vet about to fetch the bolt gun and left the room without a word.

Naturally, I took this as motivation. That night, I added a tab titled Inspirational Quotes. It featured such gems as:

Pain Is Temporary, But So Is Money.

Nothing Worth Doing Comes With Free Returns.

Excel Never Lies, Except When You Enter the Data.

I sat back, admired the glowing screen, and felt the sort of pride usually reserved for dictators unveiling public statues of themselves. There it was — twelve glorious tabs of delusion, paranoia, and financial ruin. A digital shrine to midlife panic.

I stared at my creation, convinced I'd achieved a new level of focus — the kind reserved for elite athletes and deeply unwell tax auditors.

When I finally closed the laptop, I experienced the warm, self-satisfied glow of a man who had achieved absolutely nothing — but had, at least, made a colour-coded PowerPoint about it.

And if that isn't the true spirit of triathlon, I don't know what is.

PART 3: Panic at the Poolside

Chapter 10: Chlorine and Chaos

It wasn't that I feared swimming, you understand. No, no — fear implies a healthy respect for survival. My relationship with swimming was more philosophical: I didn't believe in it. I had, however, a firm suspicion that if left unsupervised in water for longer than a sneeze, I'd simply plummet like a homesick piano.

In preparation for this aquatic debacle, I spent the week reading articles so morale-crushing they could double as breakup letters. Titles such as "Why Adults Sink: Common Technique Mistakes" and "Front Crawl for the Terminally Inept." Each one as reassuring as a clown at a funeral. By Thursday, my confidence was eroding faster than the glue on my swim goggles.

But this was IRONMAN training — and if there's one thing I've proven consistently, it's that my capacity for public embarrassment transcends both land and sea. Humiliation, I've found, is amphibious.

Porthcawl Leisure Centre loomed ahead, a concrete mausoleum dedicated to "fun and fitness" and the lingering scent of failure and Lynx Africa. A cheerful blue sign declared, "Fun for All Ages!"

I'd already rehearsed a full Broadway medley of excuses: slipped disc, rare chlorine allergy, spontaneous conversion to a religion that forbids buoyancy. Sadly, even I didn't buy them.

I checked my bag compulsively: towel (check), goggles (check), overpriced anti-fog spray I bought after reading a review that began, "Saved my marriage!" (tragically, check).

"You're prepared," I whispered to myself — a lie so audacious it deserved its own BAFTA.

Meanwhile, my brain broadcast a steady playlist of doom:
– You can't swim.
– Everyone will watch you drown.
– You'll sneeze and rupture a hamstring.
– You should've taken up chess.

Eventually, I peeled myself out of the car like a man emerging from witness protection.

Inside, the teenage receptionist regarded me with the warmth of a parking warden. "Sign the waiver," she droned, handing me a clipboard.

A waiver. For a swimming pool. What were they expecting? Shark attack? Dismemberment? Existential collapse?

The fine print read: "Management not responsible for injury, property loss, or general disappointment." Targeted.

I signed with the resignation of a man whose life insurance premium was about to skyrocket. Behind me, a poster of a beaming pensioner in a swim cap chirped, "Find Your Fitness at Any Age!" Yes, I thought. Even the age where your hips sound like bubble wrap.

Two men in matching triathlon club hoodies discussed "Zone 2 heart rate" with the intensity of surgeons.
"Zone 2, bro. Keep it easy."
"My easy is your warm-up."
I nodded sagely, pretending to understand, while privately wondering if "Zone 2" was a car park or an area of emotional detachment.

Then came the vending machine. A shrine, energy gels, Lucozade, and a protein bar called Endurance Maxx, which looked like something astronauts reject on moral grounds. I told myself I didn't need it.

I bought one anyway. Obviously.

The men's changing room smelled like war crimes — a mix of damp towels, cheap deodorant, and unrealised potential. I walked in just as a man attempted to towel himself dry with such violence he nearly achieved flight. A toddler sprinted past wearing only armbands and defiance.

I chose locker 42 because it said "ENTER AT OWN RISK," which felt like destiny.

My swim shorts, made of some malevolent polymer, clung to me like a film of shame. My heart was pounding out the entire Phil Collins discography. My brain opened five hundred tabs and crashed immediately.

The "performance grade" swim cap I'd purchased rolled itself into a sad rubber omelette on my forehead. By the third attempt, I resembled a startled condom.

At the sinks, a bronzed Adonis with pecs like a relief map of the Andes glanced over.
"First time?" he asked.
"Is it obvious?"
"You look like you're walking into your own funeral."
"Good," I said. "I brought flowers."

The pool itself was an aquatic war zone. Children screamed. Inflatable whales flew. Three elderly women aqua-jogged with military precision — the synchronized assassins of the shallow end. A man in tiny racing jammers stretched as though preparing to birth a planet.

And then there was the lifeguard.

A blond vision of smug youth, sunglasses perched on his head like he'd just finished filming a boy band music video. He twirled his whistle with the authority of someone who's never known failure.

"Excuse me," I said, clinging to my towel like a comfort animal. "Just checking which lane is for people who, uh, can't swim properly."

He blinked. "You mean beginners?"
"More like... ambitious sinkers."
He nodded, unimpressed. "Lane Four. Stay near the wall."
"Excellent advice."

"And if you pass out, try to do it where I can see you."
Comforting.

I attempted a confident stride to Lane Four, immediately executing a perfect impression of Bambi on ice. My towel leapt heroically into the pool.

"Careful," said the lifeguard, without looking up. "Pool's wet."
Thank you, Socrates.

I dipped a toe into the water. The temperature was somewhere between cryogenic and medieval punishment.

"It won't get warmer if you stare at it," the lifeguard called.
I slid in with all the grace of a dropped meatloaf. The splash could've launched a tsunami warning in Cardiff.

My goggles filled instantly. "You okay?" the lifeguard shouted.
I made a noise halfway between a cough and a foghorn.
"I'll take that as a yes," he said.

Clinging to the wall like a shipwrecked accountant, I watched the woman in the next lane perform a flawless tumble turn and shoot off like a torpedo. Inspired, I pushed off too. Three strokes in, I forgot to breathe and surfaced gasping like a duck baptised against its will.

A toddler in a float passed me, watching with scientific fascination.

I switched to breaststroke, which quickly devolved into some sort of flailing interpretive dance.

"Relax your shoulders," the lifeguard called.
"I'm so relaxed," I rasped, "I've lost consciousness."
"You're doing great."
"I'm about as great as a hedgehog on a waterslide."

Reaching the wall, I attempted a turn. What followed was less flip-turn and more exorcism. I rebounded off the tiles like a disoriented seal.

Halfway back, I drifted into Lane Three and was flattened by a man doing butterfly like he was trying to drain the pool. I resurfaced, coughing up half of Porthcawl.

"Lane Four," the lifeguard reminded me.
"Yes," I gasped, "I'm... networking."

After six traumatic lengths, I was done. Arms like linguine, lungs on strike. I reached for the pool's edge but found it receding like hope. My third attempt to climb out produced a sound audible to dogs.

"Need a hand?" the lifeguard asked.
"No, no," I wheezed. "Just... stretching."
"Right," he said, watching me ooze onto the tiles like an abandoned flan. "Graceful."

I lay there, contemplating faking my own death.
"Welcome to training," he said.
"Do I get a medal?"
"You can have a biscuit if you make it to the changing room."
"Deal."

I staggered toward the showers, which operated on a strict policy of pain or frostbite. Beside me, a man shaped like a Greek myth lathered up with something called Recovery Wash. I used a free hotel shampoo sachet that smelled faintly of car wax.

My towel, the size of a postage stamp, absorbed nothing. My shorts clung like desperate relatives at a funeral. Each time I bent to retrieve my clothes, the locker door creaked open to smack me in the head, presumably to remind me who was in charge.

My attempt to put on a T-shirt resulted in partial strangulation. My flip-flops went on the wrong feet, but at that point I respected their initiative.

I limped past the mirror, avoiding eye contact with the damp sea cucumber reflected back at me.

"Walk tall," I told myself.
I squeaked audibly.

At the exit, a kindly pensioner in a pink cap gave me a thumbs-up so full of pity it could've qualified as charity work. I nodded, shuffled out, and emerged into the car park reborn — damp, humbled, and smelling faintly of chemical failure.

The drive home was silent, save for the wet squelch of polyester and poor life planning. The car windows fogged with quiet acceptance.

7:02 a.m. Not even breakfast, and I'd already performed public slapstick for an audience of toddlers and lifeguards.

I texted Dan.
Me: First swim done.
Dan: Did you drown?
Me: Nearly. Lifeguard knows my name now.
Dan: Progress?
Me: Like a Labrador in a kiddie pool. Half drowned, half proud.
Dan: Pub tonight?
Me: Obviously.

I stared at the message thread, water still dripping off my ear.

Surely it could only improve from here.

It had to.

Didn't it?

Chapter 11: Kit Shame and Saddle Pain

There was a moment — a short, shimmering moment — when I stepped out of the bedroom wearing my new "performance" running vest and Connie looked at me the way one might look at a man who had politely asked if he could attend your wedding dressed as a condom.

She said nothing at first. The silence was profound. The kind of silence that isn't empty but armed. It stood there, arms folded, radiating judgment in high definition.

"It's technical fabric," I offered, tugging at the hem with doomed optimism. "Breathable."

"Is that why I can see your nipples?" she asked, tilting her head like an art critic surveying a disappointing sculpture. "Are they... breathable too?"

I looked down. Indeed, they were. Two startled pink raisins, desperately pressing against the fabric as if trying to stage an escape attempt.

"And the shorts?" she said slowly.

"Compression," I replied. "Helps with recovery."

"Helps who recover? The people forced to look at you?"

Even the dog couldn't bear witness. Bella sighed, loudly, from the depths of her soul — a sound that conveyed not just pity, but regret for having been domesticated — and padded out of the room in disgust.

There I stood: £40 running vest, £50 compression shorts, calf sleeves nicked from a Marvel character, and reflective socks so bright they could summon aircraft. On my face — wraparound sunglasses promising "aerodynamics" but delivering "divorced man at Center Parcs."

The worst part? For about five delusional seconds in front of the mirror, I actually thought I looked alright. Not good, obviously —

I'm not insane — but marginally athletic, like one of those men on YouTube who offer training tips while clearly fighting off gout.

The Lycra clung to me like guilt. The running vest exposed more ambition than ability. The sunglasses made me look like a bug on witness protection, and the cap — dear God — the cap. Ten minutes I spent debating whether I looked "race-ready" or "emotionally fragile."

Still, I'd bought the gear, so there was nothing left but to step outside and hope the street could handle this much synthetic optimism.

Moments later, I was jogging down the street past Mrs Evans's house — legs flapping, stomach jiggling, dignity clinging to me like a Tesco bag in a gale. She wasn't outside, thankfully. Just her gnome, the one with the fishing rod, staring at me as if witnessing the fall of man.

I ducked my head and picked up the pace, praying no one else would see this shimmering Lycra tragedy in motion.

Naturally, I was wrong.

Mrs Loughton was out front pruning her roses. She froze. Dropped her secateurs. Then slowly backed into the hedge, like David Attenborough narrating the retreat of an animal sensing danger.

A child on a scooter overtook me — overtook me — glanced back, and shouted, "Oi! Nice banana costume!"

To be fair, the vest was fluorescent yellow. The label had boasted "Enhanced Visibility." It had succeeded — I could be spotted from orbit.

There's a unique kind of shame that comes from running past your neighbours dressed like a sentient highlighter. It's not embarrassment; it's deeper. A primal awareness that you are both predator and prey.

Still, I made it round the block once — a single lap of humiliation — enough to "test the gear" and not enough to justify therapy.

Later that week, after another ride that left me walking like a man who'd dismounted a hedgehog, I made the only logical conclusion: the bike was the problem.

Not me. Not my posture. Not my catastrophic approach to fitness. The bike.

While Googling "why does cycling destroy your undercarriage," I somehow ended up on Garmin's website — that digital temple of false hope. I'd only meant to browse, maybe price-check a heart rate strap, but the website didn't sell equipment; it sold redemption.

Sleek product shots. Glowing route maps. Men with abs like warning triangles promising, This could be you!

It couldn't. But that didn't stop me.

I hovered. I closed the tab. I reopened it. I promised myself I'd wait for a sale. Then I bought it at full price — plus the optional heart rate monitor, silicone case, and the illusion of control.

When the box arrived, Connie thought it was a new phone. Bella tried to eat the packaging. I spent the evening pairing it with everything I owned — bike, phone, ego. Two out of three connected.

Soon after came an article titled "Stop Suffering: Get a Proper Bike Fit." The photo showed a man being gently manipulated by someone in Lycra. It looked vaguely sensual and deeply reassuring.

Click. Booked.

It felt adult, like scheduling therapy for my arse.

The fitter's name was Connor, but he looked like a Blake — all swoopy hair and designer stubble. He greeted me with the confidence of a man who stretches for sport.

I'd cycled there — because irony — and by the time I dismounted, my backside felt like it had lost a custody battle.

"Welcome to your fit, mate," Connor said, gesturing to a sleek turbo trainer mounted on what looked suspiciously like a sacrificial altar. The room smelled faintly of Dettol and self confidence.

"Hop on when you're ready," he said.

I was not ready. I will never be ready.

He circled me like David Attenborough observing a dying wildebeest. Occasionally he'd crouch, poke at my legs, and mutter things like, "Hips are a bit tight," as if diagnosing a haunted piano.

"I'm forty-three," I said. "Everything's a bit tight."

He nodded gravely. "Your left knee's tracking wide."

"Good," I said. "At least something's tracking."

He adjusted my saddle height by three millimetres — with the gravitas of a brain surgeon — and declared, "That'll reduce pelvic pressure." Which, translated, meant: your arse is broken, mate.

Then came "cleat alignment," a process that involved him kneeling intimately close to my feet while I tried to look casual and not to move.

After forty-five minutes, he straightened up, beaming. "You'll feel a massive difference!"

I did. Mostly in my will to live.

I paid, smiled, and left walking like I'd just auditioned for a cowboy remake of Swan Lake.

Back home, I collapsed into a chair. The ache was... specific. Not the general hum of middle age, but a deep, personal pain radiating from regions one usually reserves for sitting quietly.

This was supposed to help. The bike fit. The new bib shorts. The saddle "scientifically designed to protect sensitive zones." Instead, I found myself applying frozen peas to areas not previously acquainted with petit pois.

I'd also bought a saddle bag. Supposedly "streamlined" and "minimalist." Once I'd filled it, however, it resembled a small suitcase clinging desperately to my bike's undercarriage.

I'd laid everything out on the table like an anxious boy scout: multi-tool, spare tube, tyre levers, an energy gel with the texture of wallpaper paste and the flavour of vengeance, two dog poo bags (for reasons), and an Allen key small enough to fix a dollhouse.

Connie walked past, surveyed the chaos, and said, "Are you planning to be rescued?"

"I like to be prepared."

"For what? A midlife apocalypse?"

I ignored her and packed everything anyway. By the time I'd finished, the bag was bulging like a python that had swallowed a lunchbox.

On the road, it rattled like a toolbox in a tumble dryer. Every bump sounded like I was dragging a haunted filing cabinet behind me. At one point I hit a pothole and thought I'd lost a kidney.

When I finally dismounted, the noise didn't stop — because it was coming from me. My joints were clicking in Morse code.

I peeled off the Lycra with the grace of a man moulting, collapsed onto the sofa in joggers two sizes too big, and lay there in silence.

Then I remembered the tub.

It sat innocently in the kit drawer: UltraGlide Endurance Cream. The label showed a smiling cyclist, the sort of man who says things like "You'll love the burn!" unironically.

I read the instructions. "Read" being the wrong verb. I saw "apply generously" and took it as a personal challenge. For context: it was not muscle rub. It was chamois cream. Designed to be applied pre-emptively and strategically, not slathered like an overenthusiastic toddler frosting a cake.

Within seconds, I was experiencing what can only be described as divine retribution. My body was on fire, but in a way that felt deeply personal.

I tried walking it off. Bad idea. I tried lying down. Worse. I tried the shower — trousers round my ankles, hose in hand — muttering "Why do people do this sport?" like a mantra.

"You alright in there?" Connie called, voice trembling with suppressed laughter.

"I think I've chemically attacked myself!"

"Is that the bum butter?"

"It's chamois cream!"

"Sure it is."

Her laughter echoed down the hall like church bells of mockery.

I emerged minutes later, half-sanitised and emotionally ruined, dressed in joggers and the aura of defeat. I lay on the bed, tingling in places that shouldn't feel feelings, wondering why every advert for cycling features smiling men and blue skies — never a middle-aged man clutching frozen peas to his groin.

I messaged Dan.
Me: Used the cream wrong. Everything from waist down feels like I'm being exorcised.
Dan: You can polish a turd, mate, but if the engine mounts are shot, all you're doing is spraying it with Febreze.
Dan: Also, stop calling it training. It's a very expensive midlife tantrum.

Before I could respond, Baz appeared, like a demonic fairy godmother.
Baz: How's the sausage casing fitting? Try talc. Or just ride naked. Fewer creases.
Baz: Or tape a sponge to your arse.

I stared at the screen, questioning every life decision since bin liners.

This sport, I once believed, would make me stronger. Fitter. Heroic, even.

Instead, it had rendered me emotionally fragile and physically al dente.

And yet — lying there, faintly mint-scented and spiritually broken — a small, deranged part of me refused to quit.

Because somewhere beneath the chafing, the shame, and the faint smell of eucalyptus, there flickered the smallest, most dangerous thing of all.

Hope.

God help me... I was starting to care.

Chapter 12: Fishguard FOMO

There's a special kind of delusion that only strikes when one is seated on a sofa in pyjamas, armed with toast crumbs, misplaced optimism, and broadband. It's that potent blend of hubris and carbohydrates that transforms "local triathlon" from something other people do into "yes, this seems a perfectly rational lifestyle choice."

And thus, there I was, chest glittering with the remains of a Hobnob, googling Fishguard Sprint Triathlon like a man casually browsing for his own downfall.

The event page appeared, glossy and full of liars — photos of beaming athletes jogging up the slipway as though seawater, panic, and the urge to vomit were all part of a casual coastal stroll.

The course looked simple enough:
400-metre sea swim.
20 km bike.
5 km run.
"Beginner-friendly," it said. "Coastal views." And, most ominously of all, "Free T-shirt."

Because nothing says impending trauma quite like the promise of complimentary polyester.

I wasn't ready, of course. I wasn't even metaphorically ready. I was spiritually allergic to the word "ready." But Fishguard was local — painfully, inconveniently local — and therefore publicly escapable only through death or witness relocation.

If I bailed, Kev would know. Baz would know. Dan would definitely know. And once Dan knew, his wife Sandra would know, and from there the news would spread through the social ecosystem like athlete's foot. I'd never again be able to buy milk without hearing, "Didn't you bottle Fishguard?"

I watched a YouTube highlight reel — pure, uncut consequences. Three men being hauled out of the sea by

kayaks, one woman shouting profanities at a seagull.
Somewhere in the chaos, I felt it: that toxic cocktail of fear, ego, and good old-fashioned FOMO. Fear of missing out.

I clicked Register.

A spinning wheel. A confirmation screen. A moment of silence in which even my Wi-Fi seemed to ask, "Really?"

Then that familiar inner voice piped up — the one that usually appears right before catastrophe.
This is fine. You're fine. You are not, in any way, an idiot.

The confirmation email arrived instantly, sealing my doom with chipper punctuation:
"See you at the start line!"
How very smug.

I dutifully entered it into my Triathlon Master Spreadsheet under the column labelled Upcoming Disasters.
Local Panic – Fishguard.

Then, naturally, I did what any rational adult would do upon signing up for organised drowning: I opened WhatsApp.

Me: Signed up for a sprint.
Stomach behaving like it's in the Olympics.

Kev: Hahahahahahaha. RIP. Can we spectate?

Dan: Tactical heckling and cod & chips? Count me in.

Kev: I'll bring camping chairs. Prime heckling position. Full commentary.

Dan: We'll station ourselves by transition. Placards. Possibly a megaphone. Definitely abuse in bucket loads.

Baz: Got a cowbell, a fold-out table, I'll make signs — loads of them, all with words. "RUN FASTER, FAILURE IS WATCHING." "PAIN IS TEMPORARY, INTERNET PHOTOS ARE FOREVER." That sort of supportive nonsense.
Let's livestream it.

Dan: Split-screen: him wheezing, us eating bacon rolls.

Baz: If I bring air horns and a vuvuzela, am I officially support crew or just public menace?

I put the phone down and stared into the middle distance — buffering, like a traumatised screensaver.

I'd expected perhaps a "Well done, mate." Maybe even a gif of mild encouragement. Instead, I had inadvertently assembled a panel show. A full-scale roast, complete with sound effects.

And yet, beneath the dread, a faint trace of pride stirred. Not proper pride — that would imply competence — more the tranquil insanity of a man who's over-tightened a bolt and decided to call the resulting crack "character."

I was committed. The optimistic equivalent of a digestive in a monsoon.

***

Connie found me later at the kitchen table, still in my "recovery joggers," engaged in silent warfare with the laptop.

"You've got that face again," she said, flicking on the kettle. "The one that means you've done something stupid."

I aimed for nonchalance. "It's only a sprint."

She folded her arms. "That's the same face you had before you tried to fix your own tooth with pliers."

"That was research."

"That was a crime. You watched a video in Russian and passed out."

"It looked effective."

"You used WD-40 and a shoelace."

"It worked!"

"You screamed, the dog cried, and I had to explain the blood spatter to your mother."

I opened my mouth to argue, realised I was wrong in every universe, and shut it again.

She sipped her tea, the silent victor of another episode of Married to an Idiot: The Ongoing Series.

***

By evening I'd graduated from panic to project management. If I couldn't be ready physically, I'd compensate with paperwork.

My race plan began with "swim pace projections" — calculated by averaging my panic threshold with the speed of a frightened duck. Then came T1 transition estimates, factoring in "sock wrangling," "wetsuit rage," and "probability of collapse."

The bike leg got its own spreadsheet: route elevation, historical Strava data (none of it mine), and an absurdly optimistic average speed of 28 kph, which I'd achieved once — downhill, with wind assistance, in a dream.

I even made a weather contingency chart:

Green: Cloudy & cool — miracle territory.

Amber: Windy with emotional rain.

Red: Apocalypse — stay home and fake injury.

I titled it Operation: Slightly Less Pathetic.

It was total nonsense. But it was organised nonsense, and in middle-aged male psychology that's indistinguishable from control.

I sat back, admiring my creation — colour-coded tabs, formulas, a wind-speed calculator I didn't understand but looked clever in bold. Naturally, I sent it to the lads.

Me: Race plan done. Includes weather matrix and emotional outcomes.

Dan: You made a spreadsheet for a sprint?

Baz: Mate, it's 400 metres. That's a warm-up, not a war. I could do that before breakfast. In February. In Wales.

Dan: True. He once swam across a fishing lake to save ten seconds walking round it.

Their mockery rolled in like the tide — rhythmic, unstoppable, and slightly fishy.

***

Sunday dawned full of misplaced optimism. The plan: early ride, short run, home by ten, then roast potatoes and the smug glow of a man holding it together.

What actually happened: chaos before sunrise.

At 7:42 a.m., Jack appeared at my bedside wielding a toy sword and a jam sandwich. "Mum says you're doing your big race practice. Can I film it?"

Connie groaned. "No filming. Let him fall off the bike in peace."

Ten minutes later, I was in the garage hunting for gloves. I found three lefts, a child's welly, the missing TV remote, and a plastic dinosaur duct-taped to a spoon. I didn't ask.

Ellie looked up from her phone as I passed. "You're going out in that?"

Jack, meanwhile, donned ski goggles and yelled, "GO DAD GO!" before tripping over the dog.

Connie handed me a banana. "Good luck, Tour de Wobble."

***

Twenty miles later I returned, pink, quivering, and steaming gently like a condemned ham. I didn't dismount so much as slide sideways off the bike and stumble through the door as if fleeing a minor explosion.

The dog sniffed me and backed away.

I peeled off my kit, stood on a spoon — again — and collapsed onto the sofa. Jack wrinkled his nose. "You smell like the dog's towel."

Ellie appeared, eyes gleaming with teenage cruelty. "You've got something in your hair."

"What is it?"

She smirked. "Looks like your last brain cell tried to escape."

I lay back, stared at the ceiling, and wondered if it was possible to complete a triathlon purely out of spite.

Connie entered, placed a mug of tea before me like a ceremonial sacrifice to stupidity, and sat opposite, arms folded.

"So," she said, "do you want us to clap or follow you in the car with the hazards on?"
I hesitated. "The second one sounds more realistic."
"Fine," she said. "I'll charge the dashcam."

The dog sighed theatrically. The children fought over pancakes.

And I sat there, legs humming, heart racing, tea cooling — staring into the abyss of my own enthusiasm — wondering just how much worse things could possibly get.

Spoiler: worse. So much worse.

Interlude: Motivational Quotes I Shouldn't Have Googled

An honest review of the worst inspiration the internet had to offer.

There comes a moment in every struggling athlete's journey when they think, "Maybe what I need is some inspiration."

Not better shoes. Not a training plan. Not to stop eating leftover garlic bread before long runs.

No — inspiration.

So, like an idiot, I opened Google. Typed in "motivational quotes for athletes." Pressed enter.

And then proceeded to scroll through the most aggressively unhelpful collection of pseudo-philosophy, gym bro wisdom, and Canva-abused typography the internet has ever seen.

Here's what I found. And what I now deeply regret.

"Pain is just weakness leaving the body."
No. Pain is your hamstring sending a strongly worded memo. Pain is your glutes saying, "We quit." Weakness hasn't left — it's upgraded to business class.

"No excuses."
Spoken like someone who's never had to train while their left calf cramps like a stress ball under pressure and their child throws Rice Krispies at their head.

"You don't get the ass you want by sitting on it."
Charming. Next you'll tell me love handles aren't romantic. I sit on my ass because I've earned it. Also, DOMS.

"Train insane or remain the same."
Or — wild idea — train smart, listen to your body, and try not to bankrupt yourself buying supplements with names like RAGE DUST.

"Run like you stole something."
I did. A free banana at the end of a 10K. It was under-ripe and I regret nothing.

"Sore today, strong tomorrow."
False advertising. I've been sore for six months and the only thing stronger is my sense of resentment.

"Success is a decision."
So is eating four biscuits before swim practice. Not all decisions are created equal.

"Your only limit is you."
Incorrect. My limits include my flexibility (none), my budget (tragic), and my bike's mysterious creaking noise that no mechanic can locate.

"What's stopping you?"
Honestly? My own self-doubt, a dodgy knee, and the fact my trisuit smells like a pond exploded inside a gym bag.

Conclusion:
Motivation isn't something you find in a quote written in calligraphy over a stock image of a mountain.

It's dragging yourself out when you'd rather stay in.

It's showing up, sore and sleepy, and doing one more rep, one more lap, one more very questionable run around your block in Lidl Lycra.

It's being the slowest in the group but still turning up. Again. And again.

Because some days, that is the victory.

Not the medal. Not the personal best. Just you — still going.

Even when the quote said not to make excuses, but your hamstring politely disagrees.

Chapter 13: The 5AM Delusion

The trouble with 5AM is that it exists. Not merely as a theoretical time on the clock, but as a bleak, spiritual phenomenon — a godless hinterland that no sane person should willingly inhabit. Its only legitimate purpose is for people catching flights, birthing livestock, or extinguishing fires.

And yet, according to the gospel of deluded fitness blogs, it's when real athletes train.

I'd read that somewhere — probably written by a man who has no job, no children, and an entire staff dedicated to pre-slicing his avocados. It declared that early rising was the secret to elite performance: "Fewer distractions, greater discipline, win the day before it starts!"

It sounded noble. It sounded inspiring. It sounded like the sort of thing said by a man who owns both a Vitamix and a moral superiority complex.

So I decided to try it.

I thought perhaps I could outmanoeuvre the chaos — sneak in a run before the school run, become one of those mythical "morning people" who meet the sunrise not with suspicion but with endorphins.

Reader, I could not.

What followed was a cinematic tragedy of failed wake-ups, stubbed toes, and caffeine dependency so severe it bordered on a personality trait. Even the dog, Bella — once a joyous herald of dawn — began hiding under the kitchen table the moment she heard the alarm.

In my mind, there would be slow-motion montages: steam rising from tarmac, breath misting in golden light, me gliding through puddles like a stoic hero in a Nike advert.

***

What I got was Monday.

Attempt One: Monday

The alarm erupted at 5AM like a seagull discovering chips. I slapped it, missed, and struck myself squarely in the face — a promising start.

I immediately tripped over the dog, who had chosen that precise moment to sleep directly in the doorway, and staggered into the kitchen producing a noise not unlike a wounded tuba. Somewhere outside, a fox froze mid-step and stared at me in horror, as though witnessing an evolutionary mistake. Neither of us were fully dressed.

Coffee, I thought. Salvation through caffeine.
Except the jar was empty. I stared at it for a solid thirty seconds, willing it to refill itself out of pity. It didn't.

I settled for hot water, which I pretended was "cleansing," though it tasted like regret brewed through copper pipes. Then came the dressing ritual — a farce of epic proportions. My leggings were inside out, my top backwards, and one of my socks appeared to belong to a small child. My headphones were missing, my Garmin was dead, and the front door lock jammed for the first time since Gordon Brown was in office.

By the time I emerged, the sun was still asleep but three neighbours were awake, peering through curtains as if witnessing a burglary in progress.

I jogged down the road — briefly — and was immediately overtaken by a woman in a dressing gown putting her bins out.

Three minutes later, it rained.
Four minutes later, I gave up.

Session time: 9 minutes.
Training benefit: Light drizzle exposure and emotional dehydration.

***

Attempt Two: Wednesday

I skipped Tuesday on medical grounds, citing the body's need for rest — and because I'd slept through my alarm, my backup alarm, and the bin lorry reversing outside like a foghorn auditioning for Mad Max.

But Wednesday, ah yes, Wednesday was going to be different.

This time I pre-set the coffee machine, laid out my kit, and even wrote myself a motivational note on the bathroom mirror: "You've got this."

I did not, as it turned out, "got this."

At 5:04AM I tiptoed downstairs, successfully avoided the dog, and drank actual coffee — progress! Dressed and ready, I slipped out like a Lycra-clad cat burglar.

The sky was that uncertain blue-grey that suggests dawn or divine warning. I wheeled out the bike, clipped in, and set off into the silent void of suburban misery, chasing the fantasy of enlightenment.

Instead, I was greeted by rain with the texture of gravel, a pothole large enough to feature on maps, and a headwind so personal I began to take it as an insult.

Three minutes in, I realised I'd forgotten my gloves.
Four minutes in, I rode through a spiderweb and performed what I can only describe as an interpretive dance of blind panic.
By ten minutes, I was muttering apologies to passing wheelie bins.

At fifteen, there came a sharp pop, a long hiss, and then the slow collapse of my dignity — my rear tyre had gone flat.

I dismounted with all the grace of a tranquilised horse and opened my saddlebag like a surgeon about to perform self-surgery.

Tools. CO_2 cartridge. Spare tube. Everything required.

I am, for context, a mechanic. I rebuild engines. I understand torque ratios and combustion.

And yet there I stood, staring at a plastic tyre lever as though it were a relic from Atlantis.

YouTube offered four seconds of advice before the signal vanished.

So I began the long, shameful walk home.
Cleats clacking. Cows judging.

A passing runner nodded at me — a sympathetic nod that said, "Been there."
No. He had not.
He was not trudging home with £200 worth of technology and a deflated wheel — symbolic of both tyre and spirit.

Session time: 16 minutes.
Training benefit: Humility, despair, and one mashed banana.

***

Attempt Three: Thursday

Thursday would be different, I told myself. Indoor training. Foolproof.

At 5:55AM, I arrived at the leisure centre. It opened at six.

I stood outside in my dry robe like a confused aquatic monk awaiting enlightenment, while a cat rummaged through bins behind me with more purpose than I had.

By opening time, three swimmers were already ahead of me — lean, competent, gliding specimens of humanity. I, meanwhile, had forgotten my goggles and only realised halfway through changing that my towel was still hanging damply at home.

I improvised with a hoodie.

The swim lasted 15 minutes, five of which were spent coughing like a man attempting to inhale the pool, two apologising to the wall I kicked, and the remainder performing freestyle so chaotic a cleaner stopped mopping to observe.

I emerged from the chlorine like a man baptised against his will.

Session time: 15 minutes.
Training benefit: None. Emotional pruning.

***

Attempt Four: Friday

Connie, ever the voice of reason, attempted an intervention. "You don't have to do this, you know," she said gently. "you're not in the military."

"But I need discipline," I muttered, tying my laces with the focus of a man late for his own firing squad.

She raised an eyebrow. "You nearly cried at the microwave yesterday."

"I was tired."

"You punched the buttons, forgot the beans were in, and whispered 'why is everything so hard' with the sincerity of a man at the edge."

"I was just—"

"—and then you crouched on the floor holding a fork, muttering 'I can't live like this' because the cling film stuck to itself."

"I'm just committed."

"To insanity, perhaps."

Nevertheless, I went.

A full kilometre. That's how far I made it before my left calf seized like a startled squirrel, forcing me to cling to a lamppost while two cats held a territorial conference nearby.

Then it rained. Again.

Then I slipped on a leaf, swore at a drain, and limped home radiating pure hostility.

Session time: 11 minutes.
Training benefit: Bruising (emotional and physical).

Later, I reached for my recovery banana — only to find it had been commandeered by Jack for a school science project. It had been dyed blue, microwaved beside a marshmallow, and labelled "Volcanic Eruption Test One."

Additional injury: psychological.

***

By Saturday, I'd surrendered.

I lay in bed staring at the ceiling like a war veteran of stupidity. My meticulously colour-coded spreadsheet taunted me from the kitchen — glowing faintly with sarcasm.

Connie appeared with tea. "Rest day?"
"I'm training," I mumbled from beneath the duvet.
She looked at my hoodie, joggers, and blanket cocoon.
"Training for a nap marathon?"
I didn't answer. The half-eaten Weetabix in a tortilla spoke for itself — somewhere between nutrition and a cry for help.

Sunday: The Reckoning

Guilt struck. It always does. I owed the schedule something — a token gesture toward fitness.

I set the alarm for 4:45AM, laid out my gear like a military operation: hydration tabs, banana, functioning headphones, charged watch, enough reflective clothing to divert aircraft.

At 5:00AM, I rose.
At 5:02AM, I tripped over the dog.

At 5:05AM, I finally left the house — resolute, determined, chewing a breakfast bar like it owed me money.

By 5:17AM, the rain was falling sideways.
By 5:22AM, I was halfway up the steepest hill in the postcode, wheezing like a broken accordion and reconsidering everything I had ever done since 1994.

At 5:31AM, a milk float overtook me.
At 5:35AM, I reached the summit and emitted a triumphant squeak — which startled a squirrel and set off a car alarm.

I ran home soaked, trembling, and somehow... proud.
I'd done it. Badly. But done it.

And then, as I crossed the threshold, my shoe betrayed me. One step, and I went down like a sack of damp laundry.

The dog appeared immediately, tilted her head, and sneezed directly into my open mouth.

***

Connie arrived seconds later. "You alright?"

I raised a thumb from the floor. "I trained."

She smirked. "That what we're calling it?"

"I ran. In the rain. Before sunrise."

"Congratulations," she said, handing me a towel. "You've unlocked the Idiot Badge."

Jack wandered in, surveyed the wreckage. "Did you win?"

"Sort of," I said.

He handed me half a Rice Krispie square — my medal, apparently — and toddled off.

I lay there, dripping onto the tiles, clutching my soggy prize.

It wasn't much.
But it was something.

Chapter 14: Tri Club Induction

There's a very specific terror that strikes only when you're standing in a car park at dusk holding a swim bag, pretending you know where you're going. Not fight-or-flight terror—more the modern, middle-class dread of being underdressed, over-optimistic, and surrounded by people who casually say "brick session" without blushing.

Rewind three days. The culprit wasn't fate; it was spreadsheet guilt. I'd been staring at the colour-coded tabs in my IRONMAN file, accomplishing nothing except silent panic in 12-point Arial. The box labelled Join a Club had sat unticked for weeks. Past-me had conditionally formatted it to glow red after six weeks. Past-me is a sadist.

So I googled "triathlon club near me." Options were either 45 minutes away and staffed by men sculpted from whey protein—or suspiciously local. Porthcawl Triathlon Club.

The homepage slapped me with positivity: medal-heavy smiles, people drenched in seawater and self-regard, slogans like Push Harder, Go Further, Regret Nothing! and Sunday = Long Ride, Not Roast Potatoes. There was even a slow-mo group swim that made cold thrashing look poetic. One man high-fived a wave. I hated him and wanted to be him.

I clicked around like I was on Hinge: curious, cautious, aware I wasn't their type. Join Us beckoned. Friendly note from the secretary. Free trial. Waiver asking for emergency contact, medical history, and—essentially—any allergies to "suffering."

I hovered for six minutes, typed "Working towards my first race" under Previous Experience (no jokes, just truth), and hit Submit.

Welcome to Porthcawl Tri Club! pinged back immediately — cheery, efficient, slightly smug. Attached: schedule, kit list, and a note about "group support and post-session socials." Horrifying. Encouraging. Both.

***

The night before my first session I felt... not dread. Not quite. More the tentative optimism of a man who's bought the wrong size wetsuit but thinks, "Maybe." I laid out goggles that mostly didn't leak, a towel that wasn't crusty, and a swim cap I could now don without swearing. On top: a T-shirt that Connie bought me for my birthday — JUST TRI YOUR BEST — once a joke, now suspiciously sincere.

I'd triple-checked the PDF: 7:30pm sharp. Arrive early, hydrated, optional warm-up, bring "a positive attitude," which felt ambitious for a Tuesday. I weighed up wearing the fancy watch—the one that measures pace, HR, VO_2 max and self-esteem. Normally I avoid it in case it diagnoses me with "sedentary tendencies," but tonight I wanted to look vaguely competent.

"Are you going," Connie asked, flicking a sock into the basket, "or just arranging your excuses alphabetically?"

"I'm building up to it."

"Well build faster. Greatness and pool bookings don't wait."

***

I arrived at 6:52pm, naturally—too early to blend, too late to flee. I sat in the car watching the herd: tri suits, branded kit bags, flasks in Tour-de-France colours. People jogged from cars to doors as a warm-up. I rehearsed saying "Sorry, I'm new" without sounding like I might cry.

Inside: chlorine, ambition, and a waft of Brut (there's always one). I clutched my bag like a Year Seven and promptly lost my towel, kept my socks on too long, and joined the wrong lane before we'd even started. A man with calves like artisanal hams redirected me kindly with eyes that said bless him.

The coach—Sarah, serene, stopwatch, posture that could level scaffolding—smiled me into Lane 1. "This is for newer swimmers." I nodded, then clocked the bloke beside me adjusting mirrored goggles like he was about to threaten a national record. He had veins. I had toast.

Warm-up lengths. Everyone else slid in like seals; I entered like a wheeled bin into a canal. There was a goggle incident. Also a nose event. It was... audible.

First 50m: swimming through syrup. Second: drank half the pool and coughed an apology mid-breaststroke. Third: a rhythm of sorts. Not fast. Not pretty. Technically swimming.

Sarah called intervals, fed back at the wall: "Elbows high." "Relax more." "It isn't supposed to feel easy." (Weirdly helpful.) We did drills and kick sets. I accidentally sipped a stranger's bottle then pretended I hadn't. Nobody laughed. Nobody rolled eyes. People just trained—focused, friendly, human. Even shoulder-vein man gave me a nod.

By the end my arms were drunk windscreen wipers and my lungs were sending Morse code for "send help," but there it was: a flicker of pride. A sliver of belonging. I wasn't good. Yet. But I'd turned up, swum, and not died. No one even called me an idiot.

At the exit, Sarah was clipboard-chatting. She glanced up. "Well done tonight. You stayed calm, didn't stop, and crucially didn't zigzag across all six lanes. That's a win."

"Felt like my arms were trying to abandon ship," I said, clutching my towel like emotional support fabric.

"That's normal. You've got a base; trust the process. Fitness will come."

"I've not really done this. With people. Or etiquette. Or process."

"You survived," she ticked something. "And you didn't drink half the pool, which is more than most first nights."

"Quarter. Maybe a third."

"Progress. You racing soon?"

"Fishguard Sprint. Few weeks."

"Great local race," she nodded.

"It's, um... a warm-up. Main target's IRONMAN Wales."

She paused—just a beat. "Big one."

"I know. I signed up by accident."

She laughed. "New one."

"Involved bin liners. Long story."

"Fishguard will give you a proper taste. Keep coming. We'll get you there."

"You coming next week?"

My towel was 60% chlorinated regret, my lungs still sulking—but she'd asked like I belonged.

"Yeah," I said. "I'll be here."

"Good. We build from there."

And—for the first time in this ridiculous saga—I felt the faintest, most subatomic glimmer of not being alone.

***

By Thursday I hovered between nervous enthusiasm and full-body dread. The run session was at the park—normally dog walkers, moody teens, and hungover bootcamps. Tonight: reflective jackets, head torches, club colours. A rave for responsible adults.

I parked far away for "breathing room," then immediately power-walked after a group like a man trying to merge into a flash mob. Everyone moved with the serene competence of people unafraid of "tempo." I, however, was pre-sweating via hoodie mismanagement: pure dad-on-holiday energy.

At the meeting point, people did hamstring swings like they owned their limbs and laughed about "threshold efforts" like that's a sane Thursday plan. I hovered at the back pretending to stretch while considering a fake phone call and a sprint-walk back to the car.

"Evening all!" called a woman, clapping. "New faces—brilliant. I'm Lou, Thursday run lead. Don't panic—we're not here to break you. Much." Nervous laughter. Unclear if joke.

Sarah appeared—messy bun, clipboard, calm menace. She gave me the nod that says both "welcome" and "brace."

Intervals, of course. Not a gentle jog; structured suffering. "Six by three minutes," Lou said. "Ninety seconds recovery. Build effort. Not a race." The group nodded sagely. A man next to me did theatrical hip swings; I attempted a half-stretch that looked like retrieving a coin without committing.

We set off.

Rep 1: survivable. I hid mid-pack, copying cadence like a drunk learning a TikTok dance.

Rep 3: still upright, now sounding like a leaky bellows in a gale.

Rep 5: numb. No thoughts, just breath, blink, and an alarming copper tang.

Rep 6: still moving. Miracles exist.

We gathered by a tree that had become our shrine. "Nice work," Lou clapped. "Grab a drink; we'll jog it back." As I leaned and pretended not to see stars, a bottle appeared in my hand. Sarah materialised. "Solid effort. Held your form—especially on the last when others 'retied laces.'"

"I considered that," I wheezed. "Didn't trust my re-stand function."

Lou joined us. "You're Ian, right? From the pool?"

"Yep."

"Training for something?"

"IRONMAN Wales," I blurted, immediately regretting the Everest-on-day-one energy.

Brows rose. Lou whistled. "Full send. Love that for you."

"I'm accidentally committed," I said. "Still catching up with my own decision."

"You'll be fine," Sarah said. "Showing up is most of it."

"And you didn't cry or fall, so that's an A* first club run," Lou added.

"Nearly both," I said. "But thanks."

Back at the car park I thanked them, promised to return, and sat in my car one shoe off, panting. Progress. People. Painful glutes.

***

I approached the bike session with something dangerously like optimism. I had been riding—sporadically, usually to avoid washing up. Meet point: a lay-by that screamed "man selling logs," now occupied by cyclists doing dynamic stretches.

Fifteen of them, various shades of aerodynamic smug. I clocked shaved legs, three TT helmets, and one woman adjusting tyre pressure with bomb-disposal gravitas. I rolled in late, breathing, with squash in my bottle and a saddlebag that jingled like petty cash.

Lou waved. "Glad you found us. We'll keep it steady." Comforting? Threat?

Sarah: clipboard (obviously). "Bike looks solid. Much group riding?"

"Tons," I said. "In my head."

She smiled. "Mid-pack. Don't overlap wheels. Call potholes. If we drop you, shout oi—we'll loop back." Retrieval plan or body recovery? Unclear.

We set off two-abreast, smooth as a school of pricey fish. I was the barnacle.

I tried to blend: match cadence, maintain gaps, don't spear a hedge. Then, first hill—everyone surged like a starting pistol went off. My lungs waved white flags.

I shifted. Then again. Then several times. At one point I spun so fast I nearly reversed time. Someone breezed past with "nice and steady now," which felt like both encouragement and eulogy.

At the top we regrouped. Lou: "Not bad. Decent line." I wheezed and thumbed.

The next 20km were pothole commentary, shouted turns, and an internal monologue titled This Was Supposed to Be Fun.

We descended like thrill-seekers with budget brakes, climbed like hungover slugs. A tractor pulled out; everyone calmly downshifted. I panic-braked and nearly became rodeo entertainment.

But I didn't crash. Or cry. And when we rolled back into the lay-by, something mythical had occurred: I wasn't last. Close. But not last. Spreadsheet me awarded a green tick. Past-me would file an inquiry.

I unclipped (nearly falling), sank the squash, and took inventory: alive, tolerated, limbs attached. Sarah wandered over. "Well done. Group shape tidy, no drama. Loosen on the downhills."

"So less death-claw, more 'gently holding a hamster'?"

"Exactly."

Lou grinned. "Back next week?"

I glanced at the verge, considered lying down permanently, and heard myself say, "Yeah. I think I am."

Because despite the hills, nerves, and near-death-by-tractor, something had flickered: not just survival. The tiniest start of getting the hang of it.

Interlude: Signs of Life

There was no fanfare. No trumpets, no choir, no cinematic sunrise dissolving into slow-motion triumph. Just a Tuesday morning when I realised, mid-toothbrush, that my legs didn't despise me anymore.

That was new. They still ached, of course — but it was the good kind of ache, the kind you could boast about in the pub, not the sort that makes you quietly Google "can you sprain a kidney by existing."

I'd survived three full tri club sessions — swim, run, and bike — and, more disturbingly, I'd gone back for more. Voluntarily. Like some misguided optimist who thought "this might actually be helping."

The spreadsheet — my cruel digital overlord — was now more green ticks than blank cells. The sight of words like "brick" and "threshold" no longer triggered the urge to fake my own death. I could even drink those electrolyte tablets without pulling a face like a man licking an old radiator.

Somewhere along the line, things had... shifted.

Not dramatically. There was no Rocky montage, no miraculous burst of competence. But the chaos had dulled slightly. I wasn't confident — that would be far too ambitious — but I was, at the very least, less catastrophically bewildered.

Connie noticed too. She didn't say much — she's not the sort to throw confetti every time I manage to get dressed without incident — but every now and then she'd give me a small, approving nod. The kind usually reserved for toddlers who've managed not to eat crayons.

Even the children were adjusting to the new domestic reality. Jack had stopped asking if I was dying every time I descended the stairs like a wounded crab, and Ellie's eye-rolls at my Lycra had downgraded from Shakespearean tragedy to light domestic satire. Progress, in this house, is measured in sighs.

Bella, meanwhile, had appointed herself my emotional support animal. Every time I returned from training — dripping, sore, and spiritually vacant — she'd greet me like a soldier returning from the front. There'd be sniffs, tail wags, and that familiar look of canine pity that said, what fresh idiocy have you subjected yourself to this time, squishy human?

I'd started developing habits, too. Packing kit the night before. Checking tyre pressures. Preparing bottles. The kind of structured routine that makes you feel competent right up until you accidentally confuse Deep Heat with anti-chafing cream — a discovery that redefines "spiritual awakening."

Still, the general direction of travel was forward.

The mornings were still too early. The gels were still vile. Domestic diplomacy still revolved around my consumption of the family banana supply. But beneath all that chaos — all the Lycra, spreadsheets, and spousal disbelief — there was the faintest rhythm.

A reluctant, sweaty, undignified rhythm. But rhythm nonetheless.

And every now and then, I'd catch myself thinking about race day. Not with panic — that's so last month — but with the mild curiosity of a man who's accidentally applied for a terrifying job and is now bizarrely open to the interview.

IRONMAN Wales still loomed ahead, vast and absurd, like a bureaucratic mistake made by the gods. It was still ridiculous. Still terrifying. But, for the first time, it didn't feel completely impossible.

Just... statistically improbable.

And somehow, that was enough to keep going.

PART 4: Gels, Bricks and Breakdown Energy

Chapter 15: Gel Roulette

There are many ways to feel like an imposter in triathlon. The kit. The lingo. The training. But nothing matches overhearing two very lean, very serious athletes discuss "fuel strategies" while your last long ride was powered by leftover Christmas chocolate and rage.

It started on the club Facebook group. Someone asked: "Which gels work best for 70.3 pace?" The replies were terrifying. Talk of "carbohydrate tolerance windows" and "pre-load vs. top-up strategies." Someone linked a spreadsheet. Another uploaded a colour-coded fuelling breakdown from IRONMAN Swansea. One bloke said he "no longer trusts gels with more than two ingredients."

I put my phone down and stared at my empty toast plate. Nutritionally, I ran on white carbs, mild dairy, and a growing sense of inadequacy.

I wasn't fuelling. I was just eating stuff. Usually in a panic. That night I drew my own fuelling pyramid in the training log margin: Base layer: Haribo Middle layer: Caffeine and toast. Top tier: Panic and electrolytes I can't pronounce.

Next morning, I ordered 25 assorted gels online. And a gel belt. And a YouTube-approved "nutrition pouch" that looked suspiciously like a bum bag for triathletes with trust issues. I also downloaded a podcast called "Optimising Gut Resilience for Ultra Endurance." I fell asleep twelve minutes in and dreamt I was chased by jelly babies screaming about fructose ratios. The gels would take days to arrive, so I tried "real food" meanwhile. Connie was out with the kids. I wandered to big Tesco, aiming for bananas, flapjacks, maybe rice cakes to look professional.

I spent twenty-five minutes in the nutrition aisle hoping for divine intervention. Instead, I got Rhys Parry from Year 11.
"All right, Ian? Long time!"
He glanced at my basket. "What's all this? Picnic for a toddler?"
I looked down. Rice pudding. Banana. Jelly cubes. Peanut butter sachets. One lonely avocado.
"Training fuel," I said.
He laughed. I didn't.
Silence. The kind where you hope a fire alarm rescues you.
"Fair play," he said eventually. "Didn't know you were sporty."
I nodded. Generous of both of us. Sporty: no. Delusional: yes. Spiralling: confirmed.
The teenage shelf-stacker gave me the pitying look reserved for uncles buying protein powder without knowing what protein is. His eyes said: Sir, this is not your world.
I thanked Rhys for the nostalgia, abandoned the avocado out of panic, and moved on.

***

Delivery day. Loud packaging, colours brighter than a school disco, and a Post-it that read: "You've got this, legend." I felt judged by the handwriting.

I laid the gels out. Twenty-five sachets, technically — the box said thirty; five were duplicates, either a "legend" bonus or punishment. The flavours were ridiculous: Lemon Zing, Caffeine Carnage, Banana Hammer, Raw Salt Fury. I opened the spreadsheet and made a column called Mouthfeel, because apparently that's a thing now. Connie walked in mid-categorisation and stared.
"What... are you doing?"
"Testing fuel options. You have to train the gut."
She raised an eyebrow. "And that requires eating them all at once?"
"No," I lied. "Phased approach."
It was not phased. It was unhinged.
I set up the turbo, lined the gels like a tasting menu, and put on my "training playlist" (mostly '90s pop and the Rocky theme).
First gel: Lemon-Lime Electro-Blast.

Score: 6/10. Like sucking jelly through clingfilm.
Second: Cola Rush with Caffeine.
Better. Slightly medicinal. Sudden urge to clean the garage.
Third: Banana Hammer.
Bad. So bad. The smell alone made Bella leave the room.
Fourth: Espresso Mocha Kick.
Tasted like burnt tyre and brown lies. Energy spike followed by mild paranoia.
By gel five I was physically vibrating. Legs spinning, brain flashing like a dodgy slot machine, muttering into my phone like a man recording final words.
Connie popped her head in.
"Ambulance or just a mop?"
"Everything's fine," I croaked.
"You've got gel in your ear."

***

Two days later, I took Citrus Surge on a test run. It had scored "Least Offensive."
At 45 minutes, I opened the sachet. It exploded. Neon syrup down my hand, into my waistband, and somehow all over my bottle.
Five minutes later, my stomach issued a strongly worded statement.
Ten after that, I was power-waddling past a dog walker who gave me a wide berth.
"Looking strong," she said. I nearly wept.

Back home, I swore off gels and tried real food next day. Two mini peanut-butter-and-jam sandwiches, wrapped in foil. Plan: one at 30 minutes, one at 60.

What happened:
Foil unwrapped itself inside my shorts pocket.
Sat on it at mile four.
Got peanut butter across lower back and one armpit.
Tried to eat the second mid-run, dropped it in a puddle.
Considered eating it anyway; decided even I had standards.
Finished with jam in my armpit.

Training stress score: 38. Dignity score: 2.
That night I posted findings in WhatsApp.
Me:
Tried peanut butter as "real food."
Now I get why gels exist.
Still not as bad as Banana Hammer, but close.
Also pretty sure I'm glued to my Garmin strap.
Dan: Tried a Snickers mid-ride once. Nearly died chewing.
Looked like I was auditioning for a safety video.
Kev: Coconut water in my bottle last summer.
Fermented. Went fizzy. Smelled like bin juice.
BAZ: You've gone soft.
In 2010 I did a "fun run" with two slices of cold pizza down my
vest.
Sodium. Fat. Carbs. Morale.
That's fuelling — and lunch.
Me: That's a cry for help dressed as strategy.
Dan: Still better than Banana Hammer.
Baz: Another race I took Jerky, pickled-onion Monster Munch,
scotch eggs, two Babybels, six Wagon Wheels.
Tunnock's Teacake in the bento box. Pork scratchings in the
stem bag for morale.
Had a pork pie fall out mid-descent — nearly caused a crash.
Worth it.
Me: Right. I'm muting Baz.

***

By Sunday, I'd recovered enough digestive dignity to meet the
lads at the pub. Dan's idea. His text read:
"Two pints. One packet of crisps. Tell us about your insides.
Bring diagrams."
Our corner table waited — Baz installed with a half-Guinness
and a smirk. Kev was late; that's his brand.
Dan waved me over.
"Alright, let's hear it. Mango gel, syrup grenade, peanut-butter
sit-down... What's next? Roast dinner in a bottle?"
I slumped. "I'm done experimenting. Back to toast and quiet
sobbing."

Baz raised his pint.

"Don't blame the gels. You've got to stack them right."

"Stack them?"

"Sweet, savoury, caffeine, back to sweet. A fuel relay. Keeps the gut guessing."

Dan snorted.

"You've never done a half marathon."

Baz shrugged.

"Still better than your gel roulette."

I frowned. "You once ate a Scotch egg during a jog."

Baz nodded. "Solid fuelling."

"You stopped. Sat on a bench. Took a photo."

"It got likes."

Dan shook his head. "You carb-load for dog walks."

Baz raised his pint. "And I've never hit the wall."

Kev arrived, dropped his jacket, and barked,

"Right. Who's talking bollocks about fuelling?"

Dan: "You are. Just by walking in."

Kev ignored him.

"That chat looked less like endurance fuelling, more like a toddler's lunchbox had a breakdown."

Baz smirked. "Ian's experimenting."

Kev turned to me. "Why the face? Did someone swap your recovery drink for printer ink?"

I sighed. "Gels exploded. Peanut butter imploded. Sandwiches disintegrated. I finished with most of in my armpit."

Kev nodded, deadly serious. "Classic rookie move. You've overcomplicated it."

Dan: "Since when do you know fuelling? You only run when you're chasing a kebab van."

Kev sipped Baz's pint without asking.

"I once played back-to-back matches in thirty degrees. You know what kept me going? One bag of Frazzles and a pint of orange squash I nicked off the ref's table."

Baz leaned back. "And somehow, I believe you."

Kev shrugged. "Never cramped. Never bonked. Scored twice in the semi. Threw up in the bin after the final, but that was the goalie's elbow. Not the Frazzles."

Dan looked at me. "And this is your fuelling mentor?"
Kev patted his gut and grinned.
"Which makes my advice pure. Untainted by success."
I raised my glass. "To bad advice."
Baz clinked. "To picnic fuelling."
Dan: "To never understanding what we're doing."
We drank.

And for once, I didn't feel like the only idiot winging it.
Maybe that's the secret. Not magic gels or perfect carb
windows. Not spreadsheets, podcasts, or sandwiches that
betray you.
Maybe the real fuel — the thing that keeps you showing up when
legs ache and confidence wobbles — is knowing someone else
sat on a sandwich too.
Yet here we were. Still turning up. Still trying. Somehow,
inexplicably, invested.
I wasn't sure I was fitter. My gut was more traumatised than
trained. But something had shifted — harder to name. I felt less
like a fraud. Not quite real... but not completely lost either.
I didn't know what came next — but for now, this felt like
progress.
And progress, in my world, deserved a toast.

Chapter 16: Brick Wall

There's a unique kind of tired that only shows up when you've just cycled twenty sweaty miles and decided—for reasons unclear even to yourself—to follow it with a run. Not a jog. Not a gentle stroll to the pub. An actual, self-inflicted run. On legs that now felt like they'd been borrowed from a tranquilised elephant.

But let's rewind.

The morning started with optimism. Which, in hindsight, was my first mistake.

I'd read somewhere—possibly during a late-night scroll through one of those terrifying triathlon forums where people post photos of their toenails—that brick sessions were essential training. Bike followed by run. Simple. Sensible. Savage.

"You need to teach the body to run on tired legs," someone had written. "It's all about muscle conditioning and mental toughness."

Another person had commented underneath: "Or just embrace the suffering. Bricks are pain. Accept it."

Naturally, I read all of this while eating toast in my dressing gown. But something about it lodged itself in my brain. Possibly in the same region that still thinks I might one day own a six-pack and understand what lactate threshold means.

So I made a plan.

Not a good plan. But a plan.

***

I started by setting everything out the night before. I laid my running gear on the kitchen table. Shoes, socks, shorts, vest, spare pants (hopeful thinking). Next to it, I'd placed my bike kit: helmet, gloves, sunglasses, a gel I didn't know how to open, and two water bottles—one with electrolytes, one with hope and water.

I even set an alarm for 6:30 a.m., thinking I'd beat the heat. Or the traffic. Or my own self-sabotage.

I was, of course, an idiot.

***

By 8:15 a.m., I was still in the kitchen staring at the toaster, trying to remember what motivation had felt like. Bella was under the table, licking a spoon I definitely hadn't given her. Connie was sat at the counter with a coffee, watching me with that expression she reserves for bin collection day and tax returns.

"You're very quiet," she said, which in our house is code for what on earth are you up to this time?

"I'm doing a brick session," I announced, like I'd just declared for Parliament.

Connie blinked. "A what now?"

"Bike, then run. Back-to-back. It's a thing."

"Why?"

"It's part of the programme."

"So is sleep. Try that instead."

I grabbed my helmet and slipped out the door before she could arm herself with a stronger argument. Or her "concerned wife" tone.

***

The bike leg was, surprisingly, fine.

Which is to say: I didn't fall off, I only shouted at one car driver, and I managed to avoid both vomiting and crying. I kept the pace easy, telling myself this was all about training the legs, not chasing speed.

Still, by the time I rolled back into the driveway an hour later, my legs were humming and my jersey was stuck to my back like a damp flannel.

I unclipped and staggered inside, where Bella greeted me with all the enthusiasm of a dog who thought she might be getting second breakfast.

Then I remembered: transition.

In triathlon, transition is supposed to be seamless. Fast. Efficient. An elegant blur of motion as you switch disciplines like a fitness ninja.

Mine was more like rummaging through a car boot sale in a sauna.

"Where are my running socks?" I shouted, sprint-limping up the stairs in cleats.

Connie's voice floated back down. "Weren't they next to your trainers? You laid everything out so carefully last night, remember?"

I found them wedged between a cereal box, shoved them on over sweaty feet, grabbed my shoes, and sprinted back outside—where I immediately realised I'd forgotten to take off my helmet.

And my gloves.

And, weirdly, my cycling glasses, which gave the overall vibe of a man who'd dressed in the dark during a minor emergency.

But I was committed now.

***

The first thirty steps were manageable. Slightly uncoordinated, yes. But forward motion was happening. Then came step thirty-one, where my thighs went into full engine failure and my calves squealed like over-tightened fan belts.

This was not running.

This was... theatrical staggering.

My legs had the consistency of custard. My lungs had defected. My stomach was gurgling in a way that felt either spiritual or gastrointestinal. Possibly both.

A car passed and the driver laughed. Not cruelly—more the kind of laugh you give when you see a newborn foal trying to gallop. Awkward. Earnest. Slightly wide-eyed. But moving.

And I was. One agonised shuffle after another, but I was moving.

***

I made it to the end of our street, then decided that was a perfectly respectable warm-up. Turned right, carried on. Past the Co-Op, where I caught a glimpse of myself in the shop window—red-faced, puffing, but undeniably upright.

For once, I looked more like a runner and less like a man chasing a bus he'd already missed.

I remembered the gel a little too late and tore it open with all the grace of a man peeling an orange with a car key. Most of it ended up on my hand. The flavour sat somewhere between melted crayon and cold gravy. By the time I staggered back to our road, I'd been out for 11 minutes.

I was soaked, foaming slightly, and had acquired a strange cramp in my right eyebrow.

But technically—technically—it was a brick session.

***

I collapsed on the hallway floor, arms outstretched, legs twitching. Bella licked the side of my face, which was either supportive or a pre-emptive taste test. Connie stepped over me, phone in hand.

"You're not dead, are you?"

"Only inside."

"What was that session again?"

"Brick session."

"You look like you've been bricked, yeah."

She walked off, already typing something.

Moments later, my phone buzzed.

Connie: Next time just throw yourself down the stairs. Quicker and less laundry.

After a full five minutes of lying in the hallway like a coat someone had given up on, I managed to peel myself off the floor and stagger toward the kitchen. Every movement felt like it came with a sound effect—creaks, cracks, a gentle wheeze from somewhere deep in my chest.

I poured a glass of water and missed half of it with my mouth.

Connie was still on her phone, scrolling calmly as if she hadn't just watched me exit the house like a hopeful amateur and return looking like I'd wrestled a tumble dryer full of bricks.

"You're dripping," she said, not looking up.

"Thanks. That's sweat. Some of it might be the gel. Possibly tears."

She finally glanced at me. "And was that worth it?"

I considered this for a moment.

"In a loose, character-building kind of way... maybe."

She shook her head. "You know you've got work in an hour, right?"

***

By the time I got to the garage, I was running on endorphins, caffeine, and whatever inner wiring allows British men to pretend they're fine when they're clearly not. My thighs ached. My hips were doing something unspeakable. My calves had entered witness protection.

I parked badly, sat in the car for a full minute, and then limped into Simmons & Sons like a man recovering from a competitive limbo contest.

Dan looked up from the reception desk, instantly suspicious.

"Alright?"

"Fine," I lied. Then ruined it by groaning as I bent down to tie my work boots.

He sniffed. "You're walking like someone's replaced your spine with coat hangers. You done something stupid?"

"Brick session."

Dan leaned back in his chair, grinning. "A what now?"

"Bike and run. Back to back."

His grin widened. "On purpose?"

"Yeah."

There was a beat of silence. Then he burst out laughing.

"Hang on," he said, pulling out his phone. "Jim needs to hear this."

***

Within ten minutes, Jim had emerged from under a Vauxhall Corsa, wiping oil off his hands and wearing the kind of grin usually reserved for lottery winners and people who witness public nudity by accident.

"Let me get this straight," he said, chuckling as he leaned against the workbench. "You woke up today and thought, you know what would really spice things up? Near-death by choice."

"I survived," I said.

"You look like a bloke who's been rebuilt by someone who lost the manual halfway through."

Dan took a sip of his coffee. "How far did you run?"

"About a mile and a bit."

Jim let out a high-pitched wheeze. "What, including the bit where you crawled back inside?"

I shrugged. "It was more about the sensation of transition. Training the legs to adapt. It's called muscle recruitment."

Jim blinked. "I'm recruiting a sausage sandwich and calling that a win."

***

Lunchtime was a blur of banter, sandwich crumbs, and tactical stretching. I tried to act casual while doing a slow-motion hamstring reach next to the kettle.

Dan watched me with the wariness of someone expecting a tendon to audibly ping.

"You've got that distant look again," he said. "Like your soul's buffering."

"That's just my left eye drying out."

He squinted. "Be honest—what's the plan if this all goes sideways? Like, properly sideways. Are we liable if you explode mid-brake test?"

Jim nodded as he passed, chewing. "Is there a waiver we can sign, or do we just throw a rag over you and pretend you're a bonnet?"

"Very funny," I said, lowering myself into a chair like I was made of recycled scaffolding. "You wait. Give it a few weeks and I'll be smashing these sessions."

Dan raised an eyebrow. "Mate, you just said 'smashing sessions' and made a noise like a whoopee cushion as you sat down. Let's manage expectations."

***

At work the next morning, Jim had printed out a sign and stuck it to my locker:

WARNING: MAY ATTEMPT FITNESS AT ANY TIME. APPROACH WITH BISCUITS.

Dan had written underneath:

Caution: Prone To Sudden Stretching and Smugness.

I left it up.

I was weirdly proud of it.

It wasn't that I'd suddenly become good at this. Far from it. My legs still clicked when I sat down too quickly, and every flight of stairs was its own negotiation. But the ache in my muscles felt different now—not just punishment, but proof. Proof I'd done something hard. Something I never used to do.

Even Jim had noticed.

"Seen you limping less today," he said casually as he passed me in the workshop. "Either you're adapting... or finally broken in properly."

"I'll take that as progress," I said, massaging my thigh with the handle of a socket wrench.

By mid-afternoon, I was perched in the car with the door open, legs out, sipping an unconvincing protein shake. My phone buzzed with a new message on the tri club WhatsApp group:

OLLIE (Admin): REMINDER: Sunday group brick session. All abilities welcome. 20km bike + 5K run. Meet 8am behind leisure centre.

I stared at it. Then stared at my legs.

They didn't scream "ready."

But they also didn't scream "no" this time.

Maybe I'd go. Maybe I'd even wear the calf sleeves again. After all, if I was going to look ridiculous, I might as well do it in a group.

I tapped out a reply:

Me: Might come along. Bring biscuits.

A few typing bubbles appeared. Then:

Ollie: You bring the biscuits, we'll bring the suffering.

Tom: He's one of us now.

Sophie: God help him.

I didn't know who Tom or Sophie were. But they seemed to think I belonged.

And, surprisingly, that didn't feel like a bad thing.

I grinned, shut the car door, and turned the key in the ignition. It clattered to life with the usual protest, like it was waking up from a nap it didn't want to end.

I got it.

We were both tired.

We were both out of alignment.

And we were both—just barely—still running.

Chapter 17: Tri-ing My Patience

It started, as all great tragedies do, with a towel.
Or more precisely, the loss of one — halfway through a turbo session that had already wrung from me the last droplets of dignity, hydration, and belief in the human project. Once draped heroically across my handlebars like a flag of intent, the towel slid to the floor in slow motion, a damp symbol of my failing will to live.

I stared down at it, too spent to retrieve it, as if it had betrayed me for a fitter man. Bella, watching from the doorway, turned away — the canine equivalent of pretending not to know someone in public.

By now, we were on Week Whatever of training. My spreadsheet no longer resembled a plan so much as the fever dream of a caffeinated toddler — multicoloured, incoherent, and deeply troubling. Each cheerful little cell represented another opportunity to cry. One shade of yellow actually induced cramps. In bold red, today's entry screamed KEY SESSION — which I took to mean "abandon hope."

The workout: one hour on the turbo, followed by a twenty-minute run.
No problem.
Except, of course, everything was a problem.

At minute 21, my fan gave up the ghost. It emitted a sound like a coffee grinder eating a teaspoon, shuddered, and died. The kitchen turned into a subtropical swamp. My glasses fogged, my dignity liquefied. I yelled something between a prayer and a death rattle. No one came.

At minute 34, I began bargaining with myself. "Just reach forty. Forty's the new sixty." I checked the clock. Thirty-five. Traitor.

Spotify, in its infinite cruelty, offered Let It Go. Again.
I didn't stop it. I was too far gone.

By minute 47, delirium set in. I swear the fridge winked at me. I'd ingested half a gel and most of my self-respect. The other half of the gel had glued itself to my eyebrow. I tried to wipe it and punched myself in the face. Bella sighed — the long, exhausted sigh of a creature re-evaluating her choice of owner.

At minute 58, I attempted a dismount that in my head was graceful. In reality, I lurched sideways into the counter and slid down it like an exhausted snail, one foot still clipped in, helmet now wedged beneath the dog's water bowl. Olympic judges would have given it a 2.3 for style and a 10 for pity.

I lay there panting, melting, and reconsidering every life decision that had led me to this tiled purgatory.

Eventually, I unclipped the trapped foot, changed into a fresh set of equally sweaty kit, and staggered outside like a mole emerging into nuclear daylight. The air had that crisp, self-satisfied chill that makes you regret owning lungs.

My neighbour, Steve, was already in his garden trimming the same hedge he's been abusing since 2016. He looked up.
"Still at it?"
I wheezed something that could have been language.
"God loves a trier," he added.

Bella followed me out, sat on the driveway, and watched me wobble off — her expression that of a witness who knows disaster but has chosen emotional distance.

My watch beeped at five minutes. I'd made it to the roundabout. Barely.

At the corner by the shop, the local youth militia awaited — five teenagers in tracksuits, energy drinks in hand, smirks cocked. They didn't move. Just stared. Predators who'd scented weakness.

"Keep it up, mate, you might finish by Christmas!" one called. Laughter exploded.
"Do your legs know what they're doing or are they just guessing?" another added.

"I didn't know sloths entered marathons!"
My personal favourite.

I carried on, my left calf threatening mutiny, my shoelace attempting suicide.

"I've seen my nan run for the bus faster!" someone shrieked.
"He's running all right — out of breath!" another crowed.

I said nothing. Not because I'm the bigger man, but because speaking required oxygen I didn't possess. In my mind, though, I flipped them the bird and imagined Mo Farah weeping with pride.

At the next junction, Mrs Carmichael appeared with her chihuahua, the local gossip with a PhD in Concerned Looks.
"Bless you," she said, as if I'd sneezed rather than stumbled past looking like a freshly drowned otter.
"Triathlon training," I gasped.
"Oh," she said. "Is that a midlife thing?"
"Apparently."
She pressed a Werther's Original into my sweaty palm — a golden lozenge of pity. I carried it the whole way home, my sweet sticky badge of shame.

By minute 11, the run had decayed into a shuffle, then a limp, then a philosophical crisis.

***

Back inside, I collapsed face-first in the hallway. Shoes on. Cap backwards. Dignity missing, presumed dead.
Connie stepped over me like one steps over a fallen tree — inconvenienced but unsurprised. She put the kettle on, returned five minutes later with a mug of tea and a towel, laying them beside my corpse as offerings to the Household God of Hopeless Men.

"You alright?"
"Hard to say."
"You look like the race director just announced the route goes up Snowdon."
"Twice," I added. "Honestly sounds restful."

She sat beside me. Bella curled at my feet, pretending I was compost.

"I nearly bailed," I confessed. "Did the bike, couldn't face the run, did it anyway. Sort of."
"How far?"
"Eleven minutes. Most of it accidental. Gravity helped."
"You still went out."
"I also got roasted by a gang of teenagers and pity-fed by Mrs Carmichael."
"Did you cry?"
"Not... properly."
"Then we'll call it a win."

"I thought I'd feel more like an athlete," I said, "less like a flan that's trying to jog."
"You do wobble with conviction. That's progress."
"Seriously, I'm broken — not heroically broken, just... wrong. Like Google Maps gave up and left me buffering in shame."

She handed me the towel.
"You remember the IKEA bunk bed?"
"Oh God."
"You swore, ate crisps, rebuilt it three times, and called the Allen key 'an insult, not a tool.'"
"Thanks for that trauma."
"My point: you didn't quit. You just shouted and looked ridiculous until it worked. Same energy here."
"This is not the same as flat-pack furniture."
"No, this has fewer instructions and worse snacks."

Bella coughed, farted, and sighed all at once. It was profoundly motivational.

***

After two showers — one for sweat, one for existential despair — I nested on the sofa: blanket, toast, tea, dog. Still Life with Idiot.

Baz: Still alive, or full DNS — Did Not Start because life got hard?

Me: Still breathing. Emotionally DNF — Did Not Function.

Dan: Saw a man limping past the roundabout earlier. Looked like he'd been chased through a hedge by a sheep with anger issues.

Kev: I've written his eulogy. Opens with "He meant well" and ends with "Cremation delayed until someone unclips him."

I typed back:
Turbo: catastrophic.
Run: humiliating.
Spirit: broken.
Toast: effective.
Me: still here.

Baz: That's the spirit! The damp, quivering spirit we admire.
Kev: Pain's just part of the membership perks.

***

Later, Connie joined me. Bella snored. The air smelled of toast and low expectations.
"You feeling better?"
"Not fixed. Just... less shattered."
"You'll carry on?"
"Of course. I just needed the planet to stop spinning for a bit."
"You're allowed those days."
"Even if I nearly cried into a sweat towel and traumatised a chihuahua?"
"Especially those."

"I checked the Fishguard race."
"Checked?"
"Confirmed I'm still entered."
She raised an eyebrow. "You thought they'd release you on compassionate grounds?"
"I was hoping for cancellation through pity."
"I'm proud of you," she said.
"Really?"
"Yes. You're stupid. But brave. Like an overheated penguin pursuing destiny."

"That's disturbingly sweet."
"I know."

Then she stared, released a gust of wind that could have stripped paint, and carried on sipping tea. I pretended nothing happened. She's definitely been on the gels.

"You'll finish Fishguard," she said finally.
"Even if I crawl."
"Everyone hurts. You just narrate it louder."

***

At 12:08 a.m., wide awake, throbbing everywhere, my phone screamed like an air-raid siren. I'm fairly sure half the street muttered, "For God's sake, Ian."

PUB CHAT:
Baz: Midnight idea — we show up in matching kit and pretend Ian's our mascot.
Kev: Already ordered shirts.
Dan: Mine says Support Crew. Kev's says Pray for Ian. Baz's just says Why?

I smiled, then another ping. TRI CLUB CHAT.

Ollie: You're doing better than you think.
Sophie: Most people wouldn't even try half of this.
Tom: Keep showing up. Also, snacks.

They weren't mocking. They were just... there.
Didn't fix everything, but it helped. Enough.

***

And I dreamt.

I was running — properly running — not dying creatively, just smooth, strong, alive. No knee pain, no wheezing like a vacuum cleaner with asthma. Just motion, rhythm, life.

Crowds cheered. Cowbells rang. Chalk slogans shouted Go Ian Go (spelled wrong, obviously). Connie was there, actually proud. The kids held a banner. Baz waved an inflatable banana. Kev yelled nonsense. Dan shrugged in disbelief.

And I kept going. On purpose. Smiling. Not because it was over,
but because for once, I wasn't finished.

***

I woke up. Quiet house. Dog snoring.
And for the first time in months, I didn't feel crushed.
Sore, yes. Worn out, eternally.
But underneath it all, something solid.

Belief.
Small.
Stupid.
Real.

Enough to try again tomorrow.
And one day — maybe — to finish.

Chapter 18: Sprint Finish

I chose Fishguard for my first triathlon for one simple reason: anonymity. It was remote enough that no one I knew would witness the unfolding calamity. The people of Fishguard would never see me again (I hoped), and if they did, they'd only remember me as that panicked man in the parking lot, screaming at a banana. Which, frankly, is how I'd like to be remembered.

I was told — firmly, by the faceless collective authority of "triathletes who know better" and with the same passive-aggressive cheer my mother-in-law reserves for Christmas lunch when someone dares to suggest store-bought gravy — that I should write a race report.

"It's for learning," they said. "You'll grow from the experience," they said. They neglected to mention that the only thing growing from this experience would be the welt on my dignity and what may or may not be a prolapsed disc from attempting to mount my bicycle like a startled moose.

The Alarm: Death by Sound

The alarm went off at 05:00. Not a gentle chime. Not a polite buzz. This was the sound of a screaming goat in a tumble dryer. I lurched upright, my back creaking like an old church pew. My eyes burned, my soul briefly attempted to leave my body, and the mattress I had slept on had the consistency of whipped depression. My spine had reshaped itself into something resembling a decorative trellis, and I emerged not refreshed but spiritually battered—as if I'd spent the night being gently rolled by sumo wrestlers wearing woollen socks.

Fuelling the Failure: The Warden's Touch

Connie—my beloved wife and dietary dictator—had laid out my breakfast with the intensity of a woman preparing an escapee for lethal injection. Her annotations on my printed nutrition plan were borderline aggressive:

"Cut banana and place in blender..."
Connie: "Peel it, you absolute marsupial."

"Add blueberries..."
Connie: "Use the actual blue cup. Not the teal one. Not the navy one. The one that looks like your IQ."

"Protein powder..."
Connie: "Scoop is inside. USE IT. This isn't witchcraft."

I blended. I obeyed. I consumed the smoothie with the reverence of a man pretending to enjoy quinoa. Then, I lay flat on the world's most uncomfortable cane couch, put on Murder, She Wrote, and waited for my body to seize up while Angela Lansbury solved another homicide with nothing but polite suspicion and a typewriter.

My daughter, Ellie passed by, cast a glance at my tri-suit, which I had laid out on the living room floor, she exhaled a sigh so weighted with contempt it nearly blew out the living room curtains.

Connie emerged from the bedroom and surveyed me like a prison warden eyeing a particularly weak new inmate. I informed her, cheerily, "I need to try on my tri-suit."

"You haven't tried it on yet?" she gasped, as though I'd just confessed to sleeping with her book club.

Rule #1 of Triathlon: don't try anything new on race day.
Rule #1, I should mention, was ignored with the defiance of a man who once ate expired mussels on a dare.

The tri-suit went on the way a bear enters a tutu: reluctantly, with squeaking. There were noises. Emotional noises. The kind of noises that echo through therapy sessions for years. Once fully encased, I looked like a failed stunt double for a seal in a wetsuit commercial. One that gets discontinued due to audience trauma.

***

Fishguard Weather: The Cruel Irony

Fishguard that morning was annoyingly pleasant. Warm. Sunny. A gentle breeze. Birds sang as if to mock me. Even the local pigeons waddled past with better posture than me.

Transition Area: Competence on Holiday

We arrived at the Fishguard Leisure Centre car park, the kind of municipal edifice built from bricks, bureaucracy, and faint despair. I wandered toward transition carrying my vintage bicycle—a two-wheeled relic with the enthusiasm of a tired donkey.

All around me: Lycra gods. Men with calves like Greek columns. Women who looked like they could break concrete with their quads. Everyone was busy doing real triathlon things: adjusting tyre pressures, applying Vaseline to parts of the body I dare not name, and lunging like Shakespearean actors in a mating display.

I fumbled through racking my bike. Which should have been simple but somehow involved my front wheel turning left every time I tried to go right. A 12-year-old Marshall stepped in and helped, as if assisting a confused pensioner crossing the road.

Swim Prep: Wet Fabric Torture

Now, here is where things diverge from the oceanic horror story I originally braced for. Because this sprint triathlon was to take place not in the wild open water of Fishguard Bay (where I may have been mercifully carried off by a seal), but in the Fishguard Leisure Centre pool.

The Pool. A chlorinated rectangle of humiliation.

This was a snake swim—a phrase which I believe was invented by someone who hates joy and believes swimming should involve sharp turns, foot kicks to the face, and the occasional breaststroke collision with a stranger's crotch.

But first: the warm-up.

A man in a whistle explained the rules. Something about overtaking at the wall, don't push off until the swimmer in front has reached the flags, and please don't urinate in the deep end.

I nodded, understanding none of it, and quietly wept into my goggles.

Swim – 21:47 (Possibly in Dog Years)

I stood at the edge of lane 5, behind a 14-year-old girl who looked like she'd been bred in a hydrodynamic laboratory. The whistle blew. She launched like a dolphin. I followed like a distressed walrus falling down a water slide.

I attempted freestyle. It resembled the death throes of a drunk squid. My form was tragic. I had the buoyancy of a bread roll. After the second turn, I was overtaken by a man wearing prescription goggles and what I believe was a tracheotomy tube. He overtook me twice.

Halfway through, I began coughing up half of Wales. Someone shouted "Keep going!" from the spectator gallery. I believe it was meant to be encouraging, but it felt more like a threat.

I eventually reached the final length. A woman with a clipboard waved at me enthusiastically, either to signify "well done!" or possibly to warn that I was about to swim headfirst into a wall. Either way, I finished. I heaved myself from the pool like a beached haddock and staggered into the corridor toward transition.

T1: A Disaster

Because it was a pool swim, there was no wetsuit. Which should have helped. It did not. My fingers were made of blunt crayons and blind panic. I dropped my bike shoes, stepped on my towel, and knocked over my own helmet. My sunglasses— already fogged—fell into someone else's transition zone, where a stern woman glared at me as though I'd defecated on her garden gnome.

I fumbled. I cursed. I eventually mounted my bike the way a man climbs a horse for the first time: with the confidence of someone destined for the emergency room.

The Bike – 1:52 of High-Speed Humiliation

Once on the road, I must confess... for the first four minutes, I felt magnificent. The wind in my face. The rhythmic click of pedals. The smooth hum of my rear cassette. I was a man transformed—a warrior of the tarmac. A Lycra-clad demi-god gliding upon his noble steed, if his steed were a second-hand aluminium deathtrap with a saddle designed by a sadist.

The road wound around Fishguard with all the grace of a drunk eel. Within moments, I encountered my first hill. "Ah," I thought, "a gentle incline to warm up the legs." This was a lie. It was not gentle. It was not warm. It was vertical.

I shifted down gears like I was trying to escape a cursed dungeon, each click a fresh betrayal. My thighs ignited. My lungs felt like they were being pureed. At one point I was overtaken by a pensioner on an e-bike who shouted something encouraging, though I was too oxygen-deprived to be certain if it was, "Keep going!" or, "You're melting!"

Downhill, I gained momentum. Glorious, terrifying, unstable momentum. My face peeled back in the wind like a dog sticking its head out of a car window. My eyes streamed. My knees flapped. I hit a pothole so deep I'm convinced I saw a coal miner. Still, I persisted.

I reached for my water bottle. Attempted a professional Tour de France-style drink. Succeeded in pouring half of it directly into my left eye. Momentary blindness. Swerve. Screech. Small child cries in background. Onward.

At kilometre 12, the road veered through what I can only describe as a sheep ambush. A small flock had congregated near a corner. One stared directly into my soul and appeared to dare me to proceed. I did, but only after yelling "Excuse me!" in a voice three octaves higher than normal.

Now full of adrenaline, protein smoothie, sheep fear, and mild panic, I approached the dismount line with unearned confidence. I unclipped my right foot, swung my leg over the saddle like a majestic showjumper, placed my foot down and— ah yes—forgot the left was still clipped in.

Time stopped.

The bike continued forward. My body rotated. My remaining dignity packed its bags and fled.

I hit the pavement like a dropped meatloaf. My elbow exploded in a gentle trickle of blood. A concerned spectator approached with the compassion of a nun. I waved him away with all the confidence of a man pretending this was part of the plan.

I stood. I winced. I limped the last few metres into transition.

T2: Shoes, Blood, and Existential Regret

T2 was supposed to be the easier of the transitions. A calm, quick exchange. Hop off the bike, rack it neatly, slip into your running shoes, and trot away into the sunset like a low-budget Rocky Balboa.

Instead, I arrived into T2 like a wounded buffalo in a wind tunnel.

My bike, likely concussed from the dismount incident, refused to cooperate. I tried to rack it, but the handlebars insisted on turning at right angles like a shopping trolley possessed by a poltergeist. Eventually, I slammed it into place using a combination of brute force, tears, and whispered threats.

Then came the shoes.

Elastic laces, I had been told, were the pinnacle of triathlon efficiency. "Slip them on in seconds!" the man in the shop had said. What he hadn't mentioned was that if you have feet shaped like aggressive scones, those seconds stretch into minutes of furious tugging, cramping, and at least one audible fart from effort.

As I bent to put them on, my left calf cramped. I screamed—a loud, primal noise that echoed across the transition zone like the death cry of a moose. A nearby competitor asked if I was okay. I replied with a noise that may have been "yes," or possibly just gas escaping.

Helmet off. Cap on. Electrolyte drink—lukewarm and somehow simultaneously sweet and salty—was taken in one painful gulp and immediately regretted.

I stood, took a shaky step, and was away… like a man attempting to flee a wedding reception without saying goodbye.

The Run – 48:12 Minutes of Wheezing Despair

Let us now discuss the run.

My legs, at this point, were little more than traumatised flesh stilts. My hips screamed. My glutes sent signals usually reserved for emergency evacuations. Each step forward was met with protest from a different part of my body. I moved with the gait of a man who'd just been shot in both buttocks.

The course itself was deceptively cruel: three loops past the leisure centre, up what can only be described as a psychological incline, round a corner guarded by a marshal with dead eyes, and back again.

I was overtaken almost immediately by a man wearing a dinosaur costume. I was overtaken by a child. I was overtaken by a woman in a skirt carrying her car keys and a coffee. I waved them on, noble in defeat.

Water station at kilometre two. I reached out, grabbed a cup, and attempted to drink. Missed my mouth. Splashed it onto my chest. Choked. Gagged. Spat it out like a disappointed camel. The volunteer smiled as if to say, "You're doing great, sweetie."

By kilometre four, my soul had left my body. I was a husk. A waddling embodiment of endurance sport gone horribly wrong. I was passed by a man pushing a double stroller and still had time to wave to the crowd. I began to hallucinate. I saw Connie. Ellie, my teenage daughter was paying as much attention to my plight as Marie Antoinette would to a bread shortage—glancing up briefly from her mobile phone with the empathy of a duchess spotting a muddy peasant from her velvet carriage—before promptly returning to the far more pressing task of trying to attract the attention of every passing git in a tri-suit with rock-hard abs and the emotional depth of a protein shake. It was, after all, the only part of the event that held any genuine interest for her. My suffering merely served as atmospheric background noise. Jack was offering the kind of moral support usually reserved for condemned men at a firing squad—cheerful, oblivious, and holding a half-melted ice cream like it was a front-row ticket to the circus. He was entirely enthralled by the event, though not by me, but rather by the man in a dinosaur costume handing out leaflets and the possibility that someone, somewhere, might crash a bike. Every time I staggered past, looking like a dying llama in Lycra, he waved enthusiastically— as if I were the halftime entertainment and he was just waiting for someone to throw a pie.

As I neared the finish line, then came "Fat Freddy."

Not his real name, but a portly legend who had been stalking me throughout the race. We locked eyes. He smiled, an innocent smile, but I saw through it. This was war.

I surged forward, driven by caffeine gels, shame, and irrational spite. I increased my pace from "wounded sloth" to "lightly threatened duck." Freddy chased. I ran harder. He responded. This was our moment. Our Chariots of Fire. Our Olympic finale in sun-scorched, sweat-drenched Welsh conditions.

And finally... finally... I stumbled across the finish line, wheezing, moist, and radiating the faint smell of strawberry electrolyte and emotional cramp.

I had done it.

IN SUMMARY:

I have a lot of work to do.
No, scratch that. I have all the work to do. If there were a to-do list titled "How to Become an IRONMAN," I am currently somewhere between "buy shoes" and "Google what the hell an IRONMAN is."

Whatever I did in this race—my pre-race diet, my tri-suit strategy, my bike dismount technique (which can only be described as equestrian misadventure)—must now be used as a cautionary tale for future generations. Next time, I will do the opposite of everything I just did—except maybe the smoothie.

Because this was not the peak. This was base camp. The muddy, chafed, emotionally unstable base camp at the bottom of the triathlon Everest.

And from here... I shall rise.
Slowly.
Probably limping.
But I shall rise.

Interlude: Post-Race Audit (Kitchen Table, 21:07)

Exhibit A — Evidence on the Table

One medal: circular, reflective, and radiating smugness detectable from space.
Race number: creased, sticky, smelling faintly of effort and mild tragedy.
Trainers: drying by the radiator; left shoe stoic, right shoe formally requesting early retirement.
Me: walking like a man recently mugged by gravity and stairs.
Finding: Completion technically achieved. Competence not included in the package.
Action: Investigate how this farce occurred before celebrating that it did.

***

Exhibit B — Witness Statements (Extracts)

Connie: "Proud of you. Also: what's the plan to make this less... near-death next time?"
Ellie (from the doorway): "I can make a TikTok. Caption: 'Dad Discovers Gravity (Again)'."
Jack (from the stairs): "Can I borrow the medal for school? You look like you're done breathing on it."
Bella: [snores; dreams of ham and better owners]
Finding: Household morale sustained exclusively by sarcasm and carbohydrates. Family willing to help if plan includes nouns, verbs, and minimal drama.
Action: Produce a plan that sounds written by a sentient being, not a motivational cloud.

***

Exhibit C — The Swim (Root Cause)

Start-line emotion: Confident-adjacent.
Middle section: Consumed more water than I swam through.
Exit: Alive. Disbelieving. Slightly pickled.

Conclusion: Not "technique problems," plural. One single, gloriously catastrophic problem, underlined in red.
Action: Replace YouTube flailing binge with an actual human coach who's witnessed panic-flappers before and carries insurance.

***

Exhibit D — The Bike and Run (Secondary Symptoms)

Bike: Forward motion achieved; corners negotiated via the power of fear and braking.
Run: Legs powered by blind optimism, residual panic, and the nutritional memory of crisps.
Finding: Manageable with practice, fewer snacks, and possibly less theatre.
Action: Continue. But remember — the sea is the gatekeeper, and currently, I'm the fool screaming at it.

Decision Meeting (Minuted)

Connie: "What would make the next one less lethal and less interpretive-dance-adjacent?"
Me: "Learning to swim like an actual mammal."
Connie: "Name it."
Me: "Open-water coaching. This week."
Connie: "Day?"
Me: "Thursday."
Connie: "Time?"
Me: "6 p.m."
Connie: "Sorted. I'll pack towels and adult supervision."

***

Implementation Notes

– Book beginner open-water session. Specify: 'Previously aquatic. Currently ornamental.'
– Purchase earplugs that actually block water instead of merely offering false hope.
– Write down three things to remember when brain panics and attempts to leave the body:
1. Long neck

2. Slow exhale
3. Reach, then roll
(Optional fourth: don't die)

***

Personal Addendum (for the notebook)

Fishguard didn't expose failure. It revealed a diagnosis.
Priority: water first. Distance later.
Success metric this week: not bravery, not pace — calm
breathing, clean strokes, no crying in neoprene.

***

Closing the Audit

Connie taps the medal once. "Evidence of potential," she says.
"Not a plan."
We hang it on the hook. The hook looks taller now, like it
respects us marginally more.
Next action: Thursday, 18:00 — lake.
Bring lungs. Leave ego. Possibly pack defibrillator.

PART 5: From Mistakes to Miles

Chapter 19: Open Water Therapy

There are phrases in life that deserve government health warnings.
"Trust me, it's not that cold" is one of them.
It appeared in the tri club WhatsApp chat at 6:42 a.m., sandwiched between a photo of flapjacks and a message about toe warmers — because nothing says "serious athletes" like people comparing snacks and socks before dawn.

Ollie (Tri Club):
Lake swim tomorrow. 7 a.m. start. Don't be late!

Sophie: Flapjacks pre-packed and waterproofed.

I read this from the sanctity of my duvet, that glorious cocoon of warmth, questioning whether muting the chat would be enough or if I should fake my own death.

Then another message arrived — privately this time.

Sophie (DM): Ian — you've done Fishguard. You can do this. Promise.

Her tone was soft, practical, and laced with that deadly optimism that can make even suicide missions sound manageable.
Backing out suddenly felt like disappointing your mum, your therapist, and the King all at once.

I checked my training spreadsheet.
Next to "OW Swim – optional" was a note I didn't remember typing:
Optional = absolutely mandatory if you want to survive Tenby.

Apparently Past Me was both cruel and clairvoyant.

Some treacherous part of my brain replied:
"Fine. But if I get eaten by a swan, it's on your conscience."

Sophie replied with a thumbs-up and a duck emoji.
Nothing says "good luck, idiot" like a duck emoji.

***

The lake appeared in the morning mist like an influencer —
serene, photogenic, and about to ruin my self-esteem.
It sat in a picturesque Welsh valley, framed by polite trees and
smug picnic benches, its surface smooth as glass and just as
emotionally cold.
Too calm. Too quiet.
It had the vibe of a Netflix true crime documentary about to
begin.

I parked, sat in the car, and stared out like a man weighing up
whether spontaneous combustion could be arranged on short
notice.

The phone pinged again.

Sophie: Warm-up in 10. Bring your bravest wetsuit face.

There it was. My execution notice.

I got out and trudged towards the water, kit bag in hand, each
step echoing "you could've been in bed" through my skull.

The others were already milling about, wetsuits halfway up,
neoprene caps in hand, tow floats clipped on like inflatable
shame balloons. The air had that crisp early-morning bite that
says: "You made a terrible decision, but at least you'll be
conscious for it."

Sophie waved. "Morning! The water's lovely!"

"Define lovely," I said.

"Colder than comfort, warmer than regret. Somewhere in
between."

She handed me a swim cap and a flapjack — the holy
sacraments of triathlon.

"Wetsuit on?"

"If I must."

I unfurled the black rubber atrocity. It slithered onto the grass like a body bag auditioning for CSI: Wales.

Getting it on was less "dressing" and more "wrestling a reluctant seal into a bin liner." By the time it reached my waist, I was sweating like a Victorian chimney sweep.

Sophie turned. "Need a zip?"

"Yes. If I try, I'll rupture something that shouldn't rupture."

She zipped me in with professional efficiency.

"Snug?"

"If by snug you mean 'I'm now my own hostage,' then yes."

"Perfect. Standard open-water settings."

"What happens if I can't do it?"

"Then you swear a lot, walk out, and we all pretend it was a tactical retreat."

That helped. Slightly.

***

A whistle blew near the jetty.
Tom, the club coach, stood atop a wooden crate in a violently coloured bobble hat, radiating cheerfulness that felt like an act of violence.

"Alright team! Out to the yellow buoy, right to the red, back to the jetty. Clockwise. 400 metres. Do one lap or five — we'll wave when you've impressed us or started making weird gurgling noises."

I nodded along, hoping my face said "injured veteran" rather than "panicking liability."

"The water's thirteen degrees," Tom said proudly. "Double digits! Practically tropical. Sarah's in the kayak for rescues — just wave, float, and don't sob too loudly."

"I bet Ian to be current record for swearing per metre?" called Lou.

"Swearing's part of my warm-up," I said. "Keeps the blood moving."

They laughed. Which only confirmed I was now morally obligated to nearly drown with dignity.

Tom finished his safety briefing, something about swans having right of way — as if I planned to outswim one — and we began the procession to the lake.

The entry point was a slipway made of slick pebbles, reeds that clung like needy toddlers, and a single duck silently judging me.

The others strode in heroically.
I followed, performing a slow-motion pantomime of second thoughts.

The cold hit immediately.
My feet screamed.
My calves seized.
My lungs decided this was a good time to reboot.

"Don't fight it," Sophie called. "Just breathe!"

I inhaled. Then exhaled in a tone normally reserved for exorcisms.

At waist depth, the suit invited in a backwash of lake water — a polite internal tsunami that made me gasp like a startled cat.

Someone glided past me, breaststroking like they'd just paid extra for spa access. I hated them so much I considered tactical drowning.

I ducked under instead.
Instant brain freeze.
The sort that makes you wonder if your skeleton's trying to leave.

Goggles filled immediately. I adjusted them with hands that no longer obeyed simple instructions. I turned in slow circles, coughing, spluttering, questioning the meaning of life.

"You okay?" Sophie called, floating nearby as serenely as a water nymph.

"Everything's gone a bit... tingly."

"That's normal. Float on your back."

I did. Stared at the pale Welsh sky. My heart stopped tap dancing. The panic dropped a gear.

"Good," she said. "Now just follow me. Easy lap."

No pressure, she said. Except for the water, the visibility, the existential dread, and the green weed that just caressed my ankle like Poseidon flirting.

"Let's go," I croaked, in the brave tone of someone about to die stupidly but nobly.

***

I began swimming.
Well — technically.
It was less "freestyle" and more "mild electrocution."

Ahead, Sophie glided like a nature documentary. I followed, creating a wake that could've powered hydroelectricity.

Every third stroke I inhaled a pint of lake. Earthy, silty, with hints of goose.

I tried technique. High elbows, relaxed exhale. My elbows were subterranean, and my exhale sounded like a plumbing emergency.

"You're doing great!" Sophie called.

"Yeah!" I gasped. "Just like a dolphin! If dolphins needed therapy!"

She laughed. I drowned slightly out of spite.

But the yellow buoy loomed closer — bright, solid, achievable. For once, I didn't feel like an intruder.
My breathing found a rhythm: one-two-breathe. Still ugly, but functional. Like a tractor ballet.

Sophie glanced back and nodded. Not condescendingly. Just approval.
It hit like an Olympic medal for "Least Likely To Drown Today."

Turning round the buoy, I felt the water lift me. My legs stopped sulking and joined in. For the first time, I wasn't panicking.
Not "good," exactly — but survivable.

When we hit the red buoy, the panic was gone entirely. Just effort. Honest, uncomplicated, bearable effort.
And me, in the middle of the pack. Not last. Not in a kayak. Not escorted by pity.

That was new.
Unsettlingly new.

***

By the final stretch, I could see the jetty.
The finishers were clapping. Actual clapping. Not sarcastic.
I touched the post, rolled on my back, panting.

Tom leaned over. "How was that, Ian?"

"Still... mostly alive."

"Looked strong!"

I blinked, unsure whether he needed glasses or an intervention. But it warmed something inside me anyway.

Sophie swam up. "You coming in or going again?"

"Going... again?"

She nodded, perfectly serious.

Some suicidal part of me replied, "Yeah, why not."

And off we went.

***

Second lap.
My arms were now attached by goodwill and soup bones.
Goggles fogged. Breathing sounded like I was siphoning petrol.
Still — I wasn't afraid.

Halfway to the buoy, a woman in a pink swim cap breaststroked alongside me.
"You alright?"

"Second lap," I gasped. "Regretting my life choices."

She grinned. "Looks like you've done this before."

I almost cried. No one had ever been so wrong in such a kind way.

Then I swallowed a fly.
Not metaphorical. Actual wildlife. Straight down the gullet mid-breath.

Cue instant coughing fit, veering wildly left like a drunken canoe.

"Protein!" the woman shouted cheerfully. "Free nutrition!"

I raised a trembling thumb and carried on, now powered by fury and insect shame.

Sarah in the kayak glanced at me, didn't follow.
That's her version of applause.

By the last 100 metres, my shoulders were running purely on nostalgia, but I didn't care.
For the first time, I wanted to finish — not escape.

I slapped the jetty post, clung, and laughed, gasping like a man reborn through stupidity.

"Two laps?" Tom said, grinning.

"Turns out I... don't hate it."

Lou clapped me. "You looked like an actual swimmer. I almost didn't recognise you."

Sophie tossed me a towel. "Next week?"
"Yeah," I said, "if I stop vibrating by then."
And for once, I wasn't joking.

At the car, I peeled off the wetsuit like a snake wrestling cling film. It stuck to my ankles like a toddler refusing bedtime.

I yanked. Overbalanced. Fell onto the gravel in what could only be described as a starfish of despair.

Eventually, barefoot and filthy, I stood staring at the car window. Hair sideways. Eyes bloodshot. Goggle mark deeper than my overdraft.
But it wasn't a loser's reflection. It was someone who'd done something stupid, terrifying, and survived it twice.

"Same time next week?" Sophie called.

"Yeah," I said. "Why not."

She nodded — no drama, no fanfare, just expectation. Because apparently, that's what triathletes do: suffer willingly and call it self-improvement.

I leaned against the car boot, soaking in the crisp air. My shoulders ached in a noble sort of way. My legs were jelly, but jelly that had opinions now.

***

Driving home, I realised it wasn't relief or survival I was feeling. It was pride.

Proper, unexpected, quiet pride.
I'd done something stupidly hard.
I'd panicked. Flapped. Swallowed a lake and a bug.
But I stayed in.

Somewhere between the weeds and the wobble, I'd found something miraculous.
Not grace. Not speed. Certainly not dignity.

Just... belief.

Not in finishing easy.
Just in finishing.

And for the first time since this lunacy began, I wasn't pretending to be an athlete.

I was one. Cold. Aching. Slightly chafed.
But one nonetheless.

Chapter 20: Coach Mark The Commander of Sweat

There comes a moment in every poorly planned journey when denial quietly packs its bags and reality moves in with a megaphone. Mine arrived on a Thursday evening, somewhere between the bottom of a family-size crisp bag and a YouTube rabbit hole titled "How to Crush an IRONMAN in Just 3 Weeks!!!"

The man in the video was smiling. Too much. His teeth could have powered a small village. He had abs, a drone, and what looked suspiciously like a sponsorship deal with a coconut water company. I, by contrast, had a hoodie, mild plantar fasciitis, and a training spreadsheet that resembled a ransom note from someone losing a battle with Excel.

I paused the video just as he did a backflip off a jetty. This was not working.

My swim sessions still involved more panic than propulsion. My long rides were interrupted by pastry stops so frequent they could qualify as a bakery tour, and my runs — if one insists on using that word — were moving therapy sessions powered by caffeine gels and stubborn hope.

Something had to change.

Baz had offered to "coach" me, but his approach mainly involved shouting "run faster" from the pub car park while holding a pint. Dan's only fitness advice was "drink water between beers," and Kev continued to believe that "carb-loading" meant garlic bread and emotional denial.

I needed actual help.

Lou was the first to say it out loud, after one of our Thursday-night turbo torture sessions in the church hall — the kind of workout where the fan drowns out your will to live.
"You're getting there," she said, squinting at me through a towel. "But you're training like someone trying to assemble flat-

pack furniture blindfolded, underwater, while being shouted at in Swedish."

"At least with flat-pack, you don't finish feeling like a trifle in goggles."

"Mark's your man," she said. "Local coach. Ex-military energy. Runs everything like a recon mission."

"Sounds delightful."

"He wears a whistle. He's never blown it. But you'll still feel it in your soul."

That night, curiosity defeated pride. I found his website — a shrine to suffering in bold fonts, plastered with slogans like "Don't wish for it. Work for it." and "Sweat is your body crying for progress." It was less a website and more a digital slap in the face.

I ignored the box asking for my FTP and swim threshold and instead typed a plea for mercy:

Hi Mark,
I'm training for IRONMAN Wales. Please help before I drown, snap, or combust.

Ten minutes later, a reply arrived:

Tomorrow. 7pm. Running track.
– M

No emoji. No greeting. Just an appointment and the faint smell of intimidation. This man did not "mean business"; he was business, in human form.

***

I arrived at the running track ten minutes early because I'm British and genetically incapable of being late for authority figures.

It was one of those community tracks with faded lane numbers, the scent of Deep Heat, and just enough surface cracks to ensure injury. A few runners were already warming up. They looked competent — the worst possible start to any social interaction.

A man stood near the start line wearing a stopwatch, wraparound sunglasses, and a tri-club hoodie so crisply ironed it could have cut glass. Around his neck hung a whistle, glinting like something that could summon Bruce Willis.

This had to be Mark.

He saw me immediately — the way an eagle sees a hamster.
"You Ian?"
"Yes, sir."
"Don't call me sir. I work for a living."
"Right. Sorry."

He looked me up and down in a manner that suggested he was mentally writing my obituary.
"Tri-suit under that?"
"No. Just joggers."
He stared long enough to make me question my species.
"Warm up. Ten minutes. Start easy, finish steady."

I nodded, uncertain whether to salute or faint, and jogged off at a pace somewhere between determined and regrettable.

***

Halfway through what Mark called "controlled intervals" — and what I called "barely surviving while my organs filed HR complaints" — I heard it:

"DAWSON! LIFT THOSE KNEES!"

It wasn't shouted so much as launched — a sonic boom of disapproval. I flinched so violently my watch paused itself out of pity.

Mark was pacing the infield like a hawk who'd just spotted an injured vole. He had the laser-focused stare of an airport security officer who suspects your bag contains something illegal and deeply embarrassing.
"THAT'S NOT RUNNING," he barked, "THAT'S SPEED-WALKING AWAY FROM A PARKING TICKET!"

Lou jogged past effortlessly. "He shouts because he cares," she said.
"I'd prefer a firmly worded letter," I wheezed.

Mark lifted the whistle — didn't blow it, obviously, just brandished it like a priest warding off laziness.
"Better," he barked. "Still looked like you were running for a bus you secretly hope to miss — but better."

***

The session was biblical in its brutality. It wasn't the running itself that killed me — it was the precision. Mark scrutinised everything: stride length, cadence, posture, and whether I was breathing like a malfunctioning accordion.

"You're collapsing through your core," he said, jogging beside me without effort. "Engage. Lift. Flow."
"Flow?" I gasped. "I'm just trying not to vomit."
"You won't vomit if you run properly."
"That feels like propaganda."

He said nothing. Just ran faster. Which I assumed was my cue to chase him like an enthusiastic but doomed labrador.

***

After the session, I lay sprawled on the track like a walrus that had lost a custody battle. Mark sat beside me and handed me a plain, label-less bottle of water — hydration so pure it might have been sanctified.

"You've got work to do," he said.
"Yes," I croaked, "I've noticed."
"But you're doing it. Which is more than most."
I looked up hopefully. "So... not totally useless?"
"Not totally."

It was the kindest thing anyone had said to me all week.

He stood, dusted off his clipboard like it had offended him, and said, "I'll email you tonight. Daily sessions. Structured. Specific. You'll track everything."
"Everything?"

"Heart rate, RPE, nutrition, mood. Bathroom breaks if necessary."
"Charming."
"You'll get a weekly review. Maybe even a motivational quote if you survive till Friday."

He turned to leave, the whistle bouncing rhythmically on his chest like a smug heartbeat.
"Oh, and Ian?"
"Yes, Coach?"
"Your hoodie smells like giving up. Burn it. Be reborn."

Then he walked off, presumably to frighten another civilian into cardiovascular compliance.

And just like that... I had a coach.
A real coach.
The kind who schedules intervals on your birthday and uses "optional" as a threat.
God help us all — but mostly me.

***

The plan arrived that evening with military punctuality. No greeting. No small talk.

Subject: WEEK 1 – Foundation & Failure Prevention
Attachment: PDF. Large. Possibly encrypted.

It opened with a quote:
"The body achieves what the mind believes." – Probably Mark

And then came The Schedule — less a plan, more a manifesto of masochism.

THE SCHEDULE
Monday: Rest. Proper rest. Stretch session. No pretending to stretch.
Tuesday: Turbo (45 mins, Zone 2) + Swim (1,400m, calm not chaos).
Wednesday: Run intervals. 800m reps. Painful but character-building.
Thursday: Swim technique — bilateral breathing, paddles,

humility.
Friday: Outdoor bike (2 hrs). Fuel. Spin. Don't crash.
Saturday: Long run (75 mins). Zone 2. Smooth, not heroic.
Sunday: Brick. 90-minute ride into 20-minute run. Mild suffering expected.

At the bottom, in bold: Track everything. Log honestly. Excuses are not metrics.

Right then. Game on.

***

Monday – Rest Day
Mark said rest was part of training. I treated that like scripture: horizontal till noon, rising only for toast retrieval.
Bella joined in, sighing theatrically as if she too had peaked too soon.

At one point I Googled "DOMS from dishwasher loading."
Result: yes, absolutely, I'm a medical marvel.

Later, I opened the gym bag again—a continuing crime scene containing two fossilised Jelly Babies and a protein-bar wrapper now officially classed as a new ecosystem.

Tuesday – Double Trouble
Turbo 45: Sweated like a pensioner at Glastonbury but stayed in Zone 2. Nearly rocketed into Zone 5 when Bat Out of Hell came on. Growth.
Swim 1,400m: Entered water without tripping or drowning — early triumph. Someone in the next lane attempted butterfly and created a tsunami; I survived. For ten glorious minutes I didn't hate swimming. Possibly progress, possibly oxygen deprivation.

Wednesday – Run Intervals
Instructions: "Even pacing. Don't explode." Which is not reassuring.
First two reps: tolerable. Third: existential. Fourth: near-death. Legs became sentient porridge. Lou breezed past: "You're holding form!" I nearly wept. Finished upright — new personal best in verticality.

Thursday – Technique Swim
Introduced paddles and humility. Accidentally kicked off too hard and nearly collided with a dolphin-kick teenager who will now remember me as that man who apologised mid-drowning. Coach said I looked "smoother" — a compliment marinated in pity.

Friday – Steady Ride (2 hours)
Ventured outdoors, where the weather and road both judged me. Rode past other cyclists and pretended to know what "cadence" means. Nearly dropped a bottle showing off, recovered like a startled meerkat. Rode four kilometres with a gel wrapper glued to my thigh; a child asked if I was melting.

Saturday – Long Run (75 mins)
Planned slowness. Adult, strategic slowness. Actually enjoyed it. Around minute 50 I stopped expecting to die. Mark jogged past, gave a single nod — the coaching equivalent of knighthood.

Sunday – Brick (90 + 20)
Transition chaos: wrong shoes, wrong socks, wrong species. Still finished. Last ten minutes faster than the first. In Ian-terms, that's sorcery.

***

General Mood:
Tired, but the noble sort of tired. The kind that makes you walk upstairs like a man negotiating peace with gravity. Left calf whimpered like a bagpipe running out of air. Right quad crackled like a crisp packet in a bonfire. And yet... not broken.

A new emotion appeared beside the DOMS: pride. Not the Instagram kind — the quiet, startled kind that whispers, "You showed up. You didn't quit."

Highlight of the Week:
Tuesday's swim — bilateral breathing without near-death. Felt like unlocking a secret level. Sarah's approving nod later that week nearly sent me into cardiac joy.

Lowlight:
Dropped banana mid-ride, executed world's slowest U-turn, and rolled gracefully into nettles like a clumsy druid. Completed ride with gel wrapper affixed to backside — an unplanned motivational sticker.

Additional Learnings:
Transitions are slapstick under pressure.
Energy gels taste like battery acid mixed with suffering in raspberry flavour.
Coach Mark doesn't sleep — commented on my swim two minutes after upload. Possibly lives in my shed.
Disturbingly, I'm starting to like the structure.

Final Thoughts:
Something's shifting. I'm waking up earlier, eating food not wrapped in foil, checking wind direction like a man in a mid-life crisis documentary.

Race day still looms like a Welsh mountain with a vendetta, but for the first time, I'm not pretending I can wing it.

I'm preparing. I'm showing up.
And somewhere in the mess of goggles, gears, and gels... I'm becoming a triathlete.

Not a good one.
Not a fast one.
But a real one.

Bring on Week Two.

***

Week 2 — Settling into the Grind

By week two, Coach Mark's plans stopped reading like encrypted torture manuals and started resembling a roadmap for suffering with purpose. I was beginning to recognise words such as threshold and tempo without needing to Google "will this kill me."

The swims were improving. I'd finally stopped mistaking "swallowing the pool" for "hydration strategy." Halfway through one set, I realised I'd gone a whole kilometre without choking, coughing, or trying to discreetly die at the wall. It was either progress or gill development.

Bike rides were marginally less like trench warfare. The flat sections became rhythmic, almost meditative — the kind of peace only interrupted by the occasional insect suicide against my forehead. Hills, however, remained Satan's practical joke. I climbed them grimly, teeth gritted, muttering expletives that would make a vicar's begonias wilt.

Sunday rides evolved into a sort of moving meditation: me, the open road, and the constant fear that any moment a dog, child, or pensioner would wander into my line and end the whole experiment with paperwork.

***

Week 3 — Confidence Shifts

Running had somehow ceased to resemble CPR performed on myself. My breathing now sounded less like an injured bagpipe and more like an exhausted human.

The family took notice. Connie and the kids formed an impromptu cheer squad — which, in practice, meant sarcasm with snacks. Ellie texted motivational GIFs mid-run; Jack appointed himself "hydration assistant," which translated to occasionally yelling "Drink, idiot!" from the driveway; Connie simply rolled her eyes and hid the biscuits.

Swimming had stopped feeling like survival and started resembling exercise. I even overtook someone, though they were mostly floating. Once, a fellow swimmer attempted butterfly next to me — a full-scale water assault — and I merely chuckled instead of screaming. Character growth.

The week's highlight came when I swerved heroically to avoid a squirrel, misjudged the angle, and embraced a hedge with the tenderness of a long-lost relative. Both the hedge and I survived, but only one of us looked dignified afterwards.

A veteran from the tri club shouted, "Hey Ian, you're getting faster!" as I untangled myself from the foliage. I smiled like a lottery winner clutching a cheque made of sarcasm. Small victories.

***

Week 4 — Race Week Nerves Creep In

Taper week arrived — that confusing phase where you're told to rest just when your brain's decided idleness equals death. My legs twitched like caffeinated ferrets while my mind replayed every possible disaster scenario: punctures, cramps, public vomiting, death by wetsuit.

I consumed gels as though they were limited-edition sweets, nearly choked on a packet, and still called it carb-loading. Packing my race kit became a military operation: each sock folded with the reverence of a flag, every gel lined up like troops prepared for sticky combat.

Family banter reached Olympic standard. Ellie mocked my obsession with heart-rate zones ("Dad, it's not NASA"), Jack demanded daily "coach updates" as if I were a Formula One team, and Connie watched the chaos with affectionate horror. She double-checked my kit when I wasn't looking — proof that marriage is equal parts love and risk management.

***

One evening, sitting amid my gear, I realised something shocking. Four weeks ago I'd been a man Googling "how not to drown." Now, I was a man who could say "I'm a triathlete" without adding "in theory."

Not ready to win. Not even remotely ready to look good doing it. But ready to race.

And that, astonishingly, was when training stopped being an act of optimism and started being something dangerously close to competence.

So yes, Abersoch is next. But IRONMAN Wales is coming. And I'll be there too — nervous, hopeful, and clinging to the thought that maybe, just maybe, I'm stronger than I look. Even if, deep down, I still feel like a bin liner — flimsy, disposable, and just praying not to split before the finish line.

Chapter 21: The Shop Floor and the Bar Stool

The pub was as chaotically comforting as ever — a hallowed hall of bad jokes, warm beer, and décor that hadn't been updated since decimalisation. The air had the thickness of nostalgia, fried chips, and mild despair. Baz, Dan, and Kev were already entrenched in their usual corner, holding court like retired war generals fighting their ongoing campaign against sobriety.

Baz waved a sausage roll at me like it was an Olympic torch. "Ian, you're late. We were just debating whether you're genuinely serious about this triathlon nonsense or just conducting a long-term experiment in public humiliation."

I slid into my chair with all the grace of a dropped sofa. "Give it time," I said. "When I make the GB Olympic team, you'll all be eating my dust."

Dan chuckled. "You'll be so slow we'll have to label the dust 'vintage.'"

Kev, ever the philosopher of low expectations, nodded solemnly. "Remember when you couldn't jog a lap without looking like a dying hedgehog?"

I smiled through the pain. "Yeah, that was a moment. Now I can actually finish a session without posing a danger to myself or local traffic."

Baz took a slow sip of his pint, eyeing me over the rim. "So what's the latest? You still following that coach bloke?"

"Mark," I said. "Yes. Terrifying man. Runs sessions like a dictator with a stopwatch. He's got a whistle I still hear in my sleep."

Dan snorted. "He sounds like a riot at parties."

"Only if the party's a hostage situation," I said. "But he's effective. Structure keeps me sane — or at least, within touching distance of it."

We drifted onto the usual pub fare — football, scandalous rumours, and Kev's ongoing saga with the bike that's been "nearly fixed" since Brexit. Somewhere between pints one and one-and-a-half, the conversation veered into everyday disasters. Baz recounted the time he fell into a hedge and stayed there until dawn, emerging like a man reborn in twigs. Dan confessed to once turning a casserole into carbon. Kev muttered about borrowing something "uncomfortable" that gave him a headache for days. None of us dared to ask.

I shared my own collection of misadventures — lost socks, misplaced keys, and the memorable evening I spent trying to unlock the wrong front door because it looked vaguely inviting. The pub, I realised, was more than beer and banter; it was a temple to humility. These were my people — gloriously imperfect, self-deprecating, and armed with laughter sharper than any coach's whistle.

***

The next morning, the familiar perfume of grease, rubber, and faint despair greeted me at the garage. Simmons & Sons wasn't glamorous, but it was honest. Every bolt told a story, and most of them ended in swearing. Training had to happen before or after hours — wedged between work, exhaustion, and whatever passed for sanity.

I was elbow-deep in a gearbox that refused to cooperate — a stubborn lump of metal perfectly mirroring its owner. Somewhere between "gentle persuasion" and "full despair," I caught my reflection in the oil pan and muttered, "Olympic distance next. Twice the swim, ten times the nerves."

The gearbox made a grinding noise that felt like agreement. "Yeah," I said to it, "me too, mate."

I fell into rhythm — wrenching, swearing, and talking nonsense. The garage was its own training ground: physical, filthy, and filled with enough banter to fuel a sitcom. Somewhere between the grease and the laughter, I felt it — the quiet shift. The bloke who once collapsed jogging to the post office was now discussing watts per kilogram between oil changes. Same banter, slightly less self-loathing.

***

A few nights later, back at the pub, the crew was already mid-chaos. Baz was in full storytelling flight, gesturing wildly with a pint as I slid in beside him, freshly showered but still faintly scented with industrial lubricant.

Dan looked up, smirking. "Well, well. If it isn't our resident triathlete. You're looking less like a damp mop and more like a dehydrated fish."

Kev nodded sagely. "Yeah, mate, you're glowing. Or maybe that's just these bloody fluorescent lights."

I took a sip of my pint. "It's been a slog, but I'm finally starting to feel like I belong at the start line — not just as comic relief."

Baz grinned. "Give it time. Soon you'll be telling us your FTP instead of how many packets of crisps you inhaled before training."

"Don't tempt me," I said. "Coach Mark's got me tracking everything — heart rate, pace, mood swings, near-death experiences."

Dan laughed. "Mood swings? That's just a Tuesday for you."

The laughter rolled around the table — that unfiltered, belly-shaking kind that makes even your bruises feel worth it. In that moment, between the jokes and the foam, I realised it wasn't the medals or finish lines that made this all matter. It was this — the people who kept me grounded, mocked me mercilessly, and made every mile somehow lighter.

***

The next morning, the garage greeted me with its usual chorus — clanging metal, revving engines, and Baz's playlist of mid-

2000s hits that refused to die. I was half-hungover, wholly greasy, and clinging to a coffee mug like it was life support.

Under a car, wrestling with an exhaust pipe that hated me personally, I heard Dan wander in mid-sandwich. "Didn't think you'd make it in this early after the pub."

I wiped my hands. "Turns out hangovers don't respect training plans."

Kev grinned. "Consistency's key, mate — even in suffering."

Baz nodded. "Fair play though. You're a changed man. All this sweating and swearing seems to be sticking."

Kev balanced a tyre on one hip like a circus act. "Yeah, who knew you had it in you? For once, you're not the one we'd bet against."

I groaned. "High praise. I'll add that to my CV."

Between grease, sarcasm, and the smell of diesel, I realised the place had shifted for me. The garage wasn't just work anymore — it was part of the training. The sweating, the graft, the sense of earning progress with your hands as much as your legs.

***

Training itself had become my full-time hobby and part-time nemesis. Coach Mark's plans were merciless — every session timed, logged, and apparently designed by a sadist with a clipboard fetish.

Some days, I felt unstoppable, others, like a damp biscuit under pressure.

Take last Tuesday: six 800-metre intervals that felt like I was trying to outrun my own bad decisions. By the fourth, my legs were sending mixed signals — "Keep going!" and "We've logged a health and safety concern."
My inner monologue wasn't helping: "Look at you," it sneered. "Running like a confused flamingo. Elegant, but doomed."

When it was finally over, I lay on the pavement wondering why I do this — then my watch beeped: best run yet.
So that's progress, apparently.

The swims were improving too — or at least, I was drowning slower. Coach Mark was obsessed with form: bilateral breathing, rotation, and something called "the catch," which I assumed was the part where I catch hypothermia. But he was right; little by little, I was flailing less and swimming more.

Long rides remained an exercise in controlled agony. My nutrition strategy was simple: eat everything, drop half, wear the rest. I'd spilled more electrolytes on myself than I'd consumed, leaving the bike sticky enough to qualify as a dessert.

Still, I logged everything — even the failures. Because progress, as it turns out, is not a neat upward line; it's a scribble drawn by a drunk toddler with a gel packet.

***

Some days, training felt almost poetic. The sun would shine, the bike would hum, and for a few brief miles I'd believe I was competent. Other days, it was pure tragedy. My knee once screamed so loudly mid-run I considered phoning an exorcist. Another time, I bonked so catastrophically mid-ride I seriously debated flagging down a taxi — then remembered no driver would willingly transport a sobbing, Lycra-clad adult with helmet hair and the thousand-yard stare of a man who's seen hell. Bonking in the tri world has a different meaning. It is when you've burned through your carbs and everything drops at once—power, mood, coordination—so you're still moving, but only in the legal sense.

Through it all, Coach Mark's voice haunted my mind: "Consistency beats intensity." Easy to say when you're not actively hallucinating about ice cream halfway up a hill.

But the numbers didn't lie. Times were dropping. Heart rate zones were stabilising. I, the man who once Googled how not to drown three times a day, was actually improving.

Interlude: The Olympic Triathlon: The Mental Mile

Race day loomed like a dentist appointment with scenic views. I played every possible disaster scenario in my head: panic in the swim, wardrobe failure in transition, or simply forgetting how to run and walking off into the sea out of spite.

The course was double everything I'd done before — double the distance, double the fear, and roughly triple the bathroom breaks.

But beneath the nerves, something steadier had taken root: purpose. This wasn't just about finishing; it was about proving that all the sweat, pain, and caffeine overdoses meant something. That maybe, just maybe, this lump of a man could do hard things without catastrophic injury or public embarrassment.

I thought of Coach Mark's whistle, Baz's relentless teasing, Connie's patience, Dan and Kev's pub heckling — every piece of it was part of the story. My story.

Yes, my legs would shake, and my lungs would shriek like trapped ferrets. But when that starting horn went, I'd be there.

Because this isn't just a race. It's a saga — a slapstick epic written in sweat and bad decisions.

Next stop: Abersoch.

But don't mistake it for the finish line. This is merely the dress rehearsal, the warm-up act, the tragicomedy before the full-blown farce.

Because IRONMAN Wales is coming.

Seventeen hours of swim-bike-run misery wrapped in hero worship — the kind of event that chews you up, spits you out, and then hands you a medal for surviving the trauma.

Abersoch will hurt, of course it will. But Tenby? Tenby will finish the job.

And the worst part?
I only signed up because I was buying bin liners.

Now I am one — thin, stretched, and desperately hoping not to split before the finish line.

Chapter 22: Olympic Effort

The night before Abersoch, I was in that rare state of being where nerves, idiocy, and carbohydrate abuse all mingle into something resembling organised self-harm.

Every book, blog, and YouTube guru had drummed the same mantra into me: "Eat sensibly. Small portion of pasta, lean protein, hydrate gently."

Naturally, I ignored them all and inhaled a mountain of spaghetti bolognese so large it could have been visible from space. I followed this with garlic bread, then a bowl of trifle "for morale," then, because morale wasn't convinced, half a baguette.

By the time Connie found me sprawled on the sofa, groaning like a beluga whale that had swallowed a trombone, she shook her head and muttered, "You'll be gassing bubbles in the swim tomorrow."

Sleep was not so much sleep as an eight-hour audition for a man dying of gout. Every thirty minutes I lurched awake, sweating Bolognese, listening to the wind outside and wondering if it was practising for my humiliation. I dreamt of drowning in custard, of being overtaken by pensioners on mobility scooters, and of Freddy — though I hadn't met him yet, he was already lurking in my subconscious like the ghost of athletic failure.

At 5 a.m., the alarm went off. Not a gentle tune, but a shriek that made me sit bolt upright and instantly regret it. My stomach was inflated like a beach ball. My spine ached like it had been reassembled by a drunk carpenter. Connie shoved a bowl of porridge at me with the tenderness of a prison warden delivering a last meal.

"Eat it," she said, "and don't even think about moaning."

I stared at the porridge. It stared back. Porridge is supposed to be comforting. This was not. This was grey wallpaper paste that whispered, "You'll see me again when you burp it back up halfway through the run." Still, I forced it down, spoon by claggy spoon, because apparently success is built on oats and regret.

By 6 a.m. we were on the beach. And what a beach it was: golden sands, waves twinkling under a rising sun, the sort of idyllic Welsh seaside morning that would make a poet swoon.

The loudspeakers crackled with announcements no one could hear, nervous athletes fiddled endlessly with bags and bottles, and the air buzzed with the kind of tension usually reserved for school exam halls. Some jogged little circles on the sand, others stretched hamstrings that looked like they hadn't been stretched since 1997. The smell of energy gels mingled with salt air, and every so often a nervous laugh or whoop cut through the low murmur.

This was it: race morning.

And that's when I saw him. Freddy.

Of course, his name wasn't Freddy, but Mark had told me for every race I do, some unfortunate soul should become my nemesis. Not through malice, not through choice, but through the sheer unrelenting spite that fuels middle-aged men to find meaning in Lycra.

He was about fifty-something, with a moustache so polished it could have been entered in Crufts, and socks — knee-length compression socks so aggressively white they could blind pilots. He had an M&S carrier bag neatly folded in his transition area, a talisman of smug domestic orderliness.

In that instant, I knew: he was my Freddy. He didn't know it. His family didn't know it. No one knew it. But war had been declared.

***

The wetsuit ordeal began. Wetsuits, for the uninitiated, are zips up the back — a sadistic design feature that forces middle-aged men into public contortions not seen outside of tantric yoga videos.

I hopped, twisted, and nearly tore my groin trying to grab the dangling cord. After five minutes of slapstick, I had to beg Connie to yank it up. She obliged with such ferocity that I yelped and saw God. Ellie filmed the whole thing for TikTok, no doubt captioning it with something like "Local Dad Fights Demon Onesie." Jack asked if there were hotdogs at the finish line. Bella turned away in shame.

The horn blew. A hundred athletes charged into the surf like heroic penguins. I shuffled after them like a broken wheelbarrow.

The water hit — ice-cold, instant shock, seawater gushing down my spine like Poseidon's prank bucket. And yet, progress. Unlike Fishguard, where I had flailed like a drunk crab, here I actually swam. Not well. Not elegantly. But forward. Pull, breathe, pull, breathe.

Ten strokes in, I thought, "This is it. I'm a triathlete."

Then someone kicked me squarely in the goggles and I swallowed half the Sea.

I coughed, choked, surfaced. To my left, Freddy was gliding serenely, moustache surely waterproofed, socks waiting smugly in transition. Rage surged.

"Not today, Freddy," I spluttered, sounding more like a man gargling seaweed.

Naturally, this meant I swam completely off course, following Freddy's hat instead of the buoys, until a marshal in a kayak screamed, "Other way, butt! That's the Bristol Channel, not the finish!"

I corrected and kept flailing. Every sighting stroke, I scanned for Freddy. Was he ahead? Behind? Smirking? At one point I was sure he turned his head and deliberately splashed me. It might have been a hallucination, but in that moment it was personal.

And then, impossibly, the beach appeared. I staggered upright, legs trembling, arms dead. I looked less like a triathlete I looked less like a triathlete and more like someone the paramedics would approach gently.

Connie clapped once, in pity. Ellie muttered, "Good grief," and went back to scrolling her phone. Jack asked again about hotdogs. Bella sniffed me, sneezed, and walked away.

***

Transition One. My nemesis. My Bermuda Triangle.

I tore at the wetsuit zip like a man trying to escape a straitjacket. It clung. It mocked me. Eventually I peeled it down, tripped over the ankle, and face-planted into the sand. Dignity: gone.

I staggered into the transition area carrying the wetsuit like a defeated octopus. I found my bike. This time, miracle of miracles, I actually remembered where I'd left it.

Wetsuit dumped, helmet on. Easy? No. The helmet fell off twice. When I finally clipped it, I realised I'd put it on backwards. Off again, on again. Sunglasses fogged instantly, so I wiped them with my towel — which had, of course, been rolled in sand. Now I was looking at the world through a beige Instagram filter.

Shoes. Socks. The talcum powder I had so carefully poured into them earlier exploded into a cloud, covering me in white dust. I inhaled half of it, coughing like a panda with hay fever. My neighbour glared as I knocked his £5,000 carbon bike while trying to sit on my stool.

Freddy's transition, by comparison, was immaculate. Shoes aligned, towel folded. A temple of smug order. I muttered something unkind in Welsh under my breath and dragged my bike out.

***

The bike course was forty kilometres of Welsh terrain clearly designed by someone with a grudge.

The first ten minutes were bliss. The hum of tyres, the wind in my face — for a fleeting, delusional moment I thought, "I'm an athlete."

Then came the hills. Abersoch's hills are less "gradual inclines" and more "geological assaults." I clicked down gears like a man trying to escape a burning lift, until there were no gears left. My thighs screamed. My lungs threatened mutiny. A pensioner on an e-bike breezed past with a cheery, "Morning, butt!"

Rage was the only thing keeping me moving.

At kilometre twelve, Freddy cruised past. Effortless. Moustache gleaming, socks pristine.

"Morning," he said cheerfully.

MORNING? I nearly keeled over there and then.

At kilometre seventeen, disaster. Chain drop. I dismounted, fumbling with greasy hands while a small child yelled, "Hurry up, grandad!" Thanks, coach.

Chain back on, I remounted, hands black with oil, and powered on.

Nutrition was another disaster. At kilometre twenty-two I tried to open a gel one-handed while climbing. Instead, I squirted it directly into my face. Sticky citrus oozed into my eyes and hair. Within minutes I was a mobile wasp attractor.

At kilometre thirty-five, I glimpsed Freddy again in the distance. Socks flashing like taunts. Rage surged anew. I pushed, muttering, "Not this time." Then a sheep ambush blocked the corner. One ewe stared me down, eyes cold, as if to say, "Not you, mate. Not today." By the time I swerved, Freddy was gone again.

The dismount loomed. Memories of Fishguard's topple haunted me. This time, I slowed early, unclipped both feet, and stepped off. Upright. Glorious.

A teenager still shouted, "He looks like he's crying!" which, admittedly, was accurate. But I was upright.

Transition Two.

I stumbled in, legs wobbling like blancmange. Bike racked. Except handlebars swung and smacked my shin. I yelped, hopped, tried again. This time the bike actually stayed put.

Helmet off — except the strap tangled in my chin hairs. I tugged, twisted, nearly strangled myself. Finally free.

Shoes. Elastic laces, they'd said. "Slip them on in seconds." Lies. My feet, shaped like angry scones, refused. I tugged, hopped, muttered, "Come on, you daft loaf!" while sweating into my eyes. Finally, both shoes on.

Socks already soggy from spilled gel, but no time to change.

I sprinted out, only to be screamed at by a marshal: "NUMBER BELT!"

Back I ran, shoved the race belt on upside down, numbers flapping against my groin. Dignity? None. Momentum? Lost. Freddy? Already ahead.

***

And then, the run.

Ten kilometres. Double what I'd done at Fishguard. Legs quivering, lungs burning, nipples chafing like sandpaper. But I ran. Slowly, lumberingly, like a cow escaping a milking parlour, but forward.

At kilometre two, my nipples were aflame. At kilometre three, a volunteer offered jelly babies. I inhaled one and nearly died, staggering along choking, shouting "SWEETS!" like a toddler on E-numbers.

At kilometre five, the heat kicked in. I muttered, "Stuff this. Stuff triathlon. Stuff Freddy."

A passing runner patted my back, saying, "Nearly there, lad." Nearly there my foot.

Spectators lined the course, shouting encouragement. Only this being Wales, encouragement came with that special local sting.

"COME ON, BUTT, MY GRAN COULD LAP YOU — AND SHE'S
BEEN GONE TEN YEARS!" roared one bloke in a flat cap.
"SHIFT IT, THE CHIPPY'S OPEN IN HALF AN HOUR!" bellowed
another, pint in hand.
An elderly woman in a deckchair hollered, "I'VE SEEN
TRACTORS MOVE QUICKER THAN YOU!"
A lad in a Scarlets jersey called out, "KEEP GOING, BUTT — WE
BELIEVE IN YOU, SORT OF!"
And from the sea wall, a teenager yelled, "DAI THE POSTIE'S
GOT A NEW HIP AND HE STILL BEATS YOUR SPLITS!"

Savage? Yes. Motivating? Oddly, also yes. And somehow, the
worse they shouted, the more I moved.

Always, I was scanning. Freddy. Freddy. Where was he?

At kilometre seven, there he was. Ahead. Socks flashing.
Moustache bobbing. Rage erupted.

This was it. This was Sparta. This was Waterloo. Freddy must
fall.

I pushed. Faster. Harder. Every Welsh heckle became a mantra.
"Catch him. Catch him. Don't let him beat you,"

My legs burned, lungs imploded, but I surged. The crowd sensed
drama — two middle-aged idiots sprinting for 184th place.

Kilometre nine. I drew level. Freddy glanced, surprised. To him,
this was just another run. To me, it was Armageddon.

I screamed internally, "NOT TODAY, FREDDY!" and stagger-
sprinted, arms flailing, face contorted.

The crowd roared. Someone shouted, "HE'S FINISHED, BUT
HE'S FINISHED QUICKLY!"

And somehow, I crossed the line one second ahead. Then
collapsed. Flat. Sprawled like roadkill.

A teenager draped the medal around my neck with the
enthusiasm of issuing a parking ticket. Connie handed me
water. "Not dead?" she said. "Show-off." Ellie filmed me
twitching, captioning it Dad Dies in HD. Jack asked if he could

swap my medal for a Cornetto. Bella sniffed me once, sneezed, and walked away.

And Freddy? Freddy didn't even notice. He jogged over the line, moustache serene, socks glowing, utterly oblivious that he had been my nemesis, my obsession, my war.

But I knew. In my heart, in my sweat, in my cramping thighs, I knew. I had beaten Freddy.

No one else cared. But I did.

And that, apparently, is what passes for glory in middle-aged triathlon.

***

Lying on the grass afterwards, legs twitching like a pair of traumatised eels, I thought back to Fishguard — the chaos, the panic, the collapse that looked like a dying walrus dragged from a leisure centre pool.

Abersoch had been twice the distance, twice the suffering, but also — somehow — twice the progress. I swam straighter, I didn't fall off the bike like a confused toddler on a tricycle, and in the run, I actually found a rival to chase instead of merely praying for death.

It wasn't grace. It wasn't glory. But it was improvement — shambolic, sweaty, Welsh-savage improvement.

Interlude: Pre-Race Anxiety Bingo

They tell you to pack your kit the night before, lay it out neatly, and drift gently into a serene pre-race slumber. Like a well-prepared monk awaiting spiritual enlightenment. What they fail to mention — what they purposefully omit, like a dodgy estate agent forgetting to disclose the sinkhole in the garden — is that your brain has other plans.

It's not interested in sleep. No, sleep is for the calm, the prepared, and the disturbingly competent. Instead, it kicks off a midnight game of Pre-Race Anxiety Bingo — a deranged cerebral parlour game designed specifically to remind you of all the ways in which you are not ready, not capable, and possibly not even human.

The rules are brutally simple: Every bizarre, irrational, yet disturbingly plausible fear gets a square. Each square you mentally tick off robs you of a further ten minutes of sleep. A full house doesn't win you a car. It wins you gastritis, insomnia, and an expression that suggests you've seen things... and none of them good.

Welcome to the game nobody asked to play: PRE-RACE ANXIETY BINGO

– "What if I forget how to swim? Not get worse. Forget. As in, someone's deleted the file. Brain goes full Windows 95: 'This function is no longer supported.'"

– "What if the water is colder than an ice bath. Colder than a tax inspector's handshake. Colder than my wife's stare when I ask if I can buy more triathlon items."

– "What if I can't find my bike in transition and just wander about in neoprene purgatory like I'm in Tesco looking for the beans? 'Sorry, have you seen a red Cannondale with personality issues?'"

– "What if my wetsuit zip jams and I have to live in it forever? Become a sort of rubbery urban myth. 'There he goes, the Wetsuit Man– still searching for his bike.'"

– "What if everyone else is secretly an Olympian and I'm the comedy warm-up act? The Mr Bean of the transition area. One bloke's warming up with dynamic sprints; I'm trying to work out which arm the number goes on."

– "What if I come last and the marshals begin dismantling the finish line while I'm still gallantly shuffling towards it? I cross the line to find a teenager with a broom and a bin bag."

– "What if I get a mouthful of seaweed and it lodges in my teeth for the official race photos? I smile triumphantly at the camera – and look like Swamp Thing after a rough night out."

– "What if I accidentally drink enough seawater to qualify as a human aquarium? Forget hydration, I'm a walking saltwater reservoir. Jellyfish could spawn in my lower intestine."

– "What if my shoelace comes undone at kilometre nine and I burst into tears? And not even subtle crying. I mean a full toddler-on-the-floor-of-ASDA meltdown. Snot, wailing, the works."

– "What if my family captures the entire thing and it goes viral under the headline 'Dad Fails: The Aquatic Saga'? Millions of views. None of them flattering."

– "What if the medals run out before I cross the line and they offer me a Cornetto instead? And not even a good one. One of those supermarket-own-brand cones that taste like a budget cut."

And, naturally, in the centre — the dreaded free square:

– "What if Freddy beats me?"

Because of course Freddy's here. Freddy, who does one training session a fortnight, eats like a raccoon in a bin, and still manages to glide through events like some sort of irritating Greek demigod. The man whose VO2 max is "probably alright" and whose race plan involves nothing but vibes and carbs —

and yet he's inevitably ten minutes ahead of you, clean, smiling, and already Instagramming his medal before you've unpeeled your banana.

Meanwhile, I'm in a corner, covered in seaweed, looking like Poseidon's intern who got fired for incompetence.

And yet, this is the process. This, apparently, is the noble path to self-improvement. The baptism by freezing, chaotic, embarrassing fire. The night before the race isn't about rest. It's a psychological decathlon of doom. A mental marathon powered entirely by caffeine, cortisol, and catastrophising.

The only solution? Rehearse your bag drop process seventeen times in your head, lay out your kit like a nervous squirrel prepping for doomsday, and accept that sleep is merely a concept. An aspiration. Like 'dry transition' or 'chafeless lycra' – theoretically possible, practically mythical.

You don't need sleep. You need resolve. And maybe a Cornetto. Just in case.

PART 6: The Longest Day

Chapter 23: Bagged, Tagged, and Mildly Terrified

We left for Tenby while the rest of civilisation slumbered—our neighbours, the milkman, and, I suspect, the Almighty Himself—under that indecisive shade of blue-grey that can't decide whether to be dawn or last orders. The streetlights flickered in embarrassment, and somewhere in the stillness I realised I was not, in fact, embarking on a pleasant seaside jaunt, but rather driving willingly toward the scene of my own public undoing.

The night before had resembled a scout camp inspection led by lunatics. Connie had the IRONMAN Wales checklist—typed, highlighted, laminated, possibly notarised—and I had the living-room floor, now subdivided into colour-coded colonies of despair.
BLUE: bike.
RED: run.
WHITE: street gear.
And, because Tenby is built on cliffs and cruelty, PINK: shoes for the 1K-long ascent from beach to transition, the so-called zig-zag path—a staircase designed by Satan after a wine-tasting.

The coffee table looked like the contents of an anxious chemist's rucksack: gels and bars imprisoned in zip-locks screaming BIKE and RUN wrote in sharpie; salt tablets rattling in an elderly pill organiser once owned by my grandmother; two water bottles pre-mixed and fizzing like experiments from Hogwarts' least employable professor. A miniature tool roll contained a spare tube, levers, CO_2 cartridge and quick-link— the AA in burrito form. Connie's clipboard glowed smugly; every box had been ticked into submission.

The pink pile caused debate. The race guide explained that these shoes were to be deposited in your pink bag before the swim so that competitors could dash up Tenby's kilometre of cliffs without shredding their feet. "Nothing says elite athlete like turning up with a tiny pink handbag," said Ellie, "Dragon-Slaying with a Clutch."

I laughed, then panicked immediately that I'd forget the bag, be disqualified, and have to explain to a stern Welsh official that a herring gull had stolen my footwear.

By the time we had wedged every bag, pump, helmet, wetsuit, three children's rucksacks, two cool-bags of snacks, and one long-suffering spaniel into the car, the sun had started auditioning for the day. I double-checked that the bike was strapped to the roof, tugged at the rack as if trying to open a bank vault. I'd seen enough online videos of bikes performing mid-motorway somersaults to know mine would seize the opportunity to escape. Connie sighed.

"If it falls off, we're turning round and going home. Problem solved."

The temptation was biblical.

I settled behind the wheel, the dashboard glowing like a nervous cockpit. Pre-flight checks commenced: Swim kit (check),red bag contents (check), blue bag contents (check), pink bag (stop laughing, it's vital), cut-off times (ominous). Coffee: engaged. Pilot: trembling.

The motorway was empty, as though the entire nation had the sense to stay in bed. Connie dozed, the children lay in a blanket knot resembling modern art. Ellie had downloaded enough entertainment to last the Siege of Troy; Jack clutched his stuffed shark and asked whether IRONMAN Wales had a water-slide; Bella the spaniel, patron saint of resignation, sprawled across my wetsuit bag and snored like a small engine.

In the hush, my mind held an unscheduled committee meeting entitled Everything That Could Go Wrong. It passed unanimously.

At a service station somewhere between cowardice and Carmarthen, we stopped for coffee. The place was full of athletes in club hoodies murmuring about cadence and heart-rate zones—the kind of people who measure breakfast in watts. My offspring surveyed the bikes on roof-racks and announced loudly which looked cooler than mine. All of them, apparently. I sipped my coffee in silence, blending into the background like an unfit chameleon among gazelles.

***

Back on the road, the traffic thickened with cars bearing expensive bicycles and fragile egos. Every other vehicle was an advert for some triathlon club or another: Essex Endurance, Yorkshire Grit, Kent Kinetics. The closer we drew to Pembrokeshire, the more I felt like part of a mass migration of self-inflicted suffering. Lemmings with Garmin watches, all paying handsomely to hurl themselves off the same figurative cliff.

Convoys of estates and vans overtook us, their bikes gleaming heroically in the morning light. I watched them disappear and wondered if their drivers felt as nauseous as I did—or whether they were listening to podcasts about mental toughness instead of an eight-year-old asking if dinosaurs could swim front crawl.

The final approach to Tenby involved small towns, rolling farmland, and tractors that seemed to have entered a personal vendetta against punctuality. We became trapped behind one for several miles, its orange beacon flashing mockingly. I stared at its rear tyres, hypnotised by their slow revolution, and imagined seeing the same view during the race—me, grinding up Heartbreak Hill, overtaken by a Massey Ferguson.
"Just think," said Connie, reading my expression, "you'll probably see this very tractor again on Sunday. Only this time it'll be passing you on the bike course."

"Destination reached," announced the satnav, with the glee of a hangman reading your name.

Tenby unfurled ahead of us like a cheerful trap. Banners proclaimed WELCOME IRONMAN ATHLETES / CROESO ATHLETWYR IRONMAN! Cafés advertised Carb-Loading Lasagne and Bacon Bap & Tea £4.50. Even the library had joined in with Quiet Please – IRONMAN Reading, Last-Minute Tips. The Esplanade bristled with half-built gantries; the famous red carpet was, for now, rolled away like a secret.

Athletes were everywhere—shoals of colour-coded ambition flitting between coffee stands. Veterans strutted in faded 2015 hoodies, displaying calf muscles that looked carved by Michelangelo. First-timers, recognisable by their thousand-yard stares, wandered like condemned men queuing for their own execution. Locals watched from café tables, sipping tea with the detached amusement of people who know better.

Outside a bakery, a woman elbowed her friend. "Barmy, the lot of 'em. Should lock 'em up."
Her friend shrugged. "Fair play, mind—we'll still shout."

Ellie filmed everything for her social media empire. "Day One: Dad arrives in Tenby. He looks like he's about to cry, but that's normal." She panned the camera toward a group of flexible men stretching against a wall. "Meanwhile, these guys appear to be made of rubber and sponsored by smugness".
Jack peered at the crowd. "Dad, everyone's legs are bigger than yours."
Even the dog looked embarrassed.

Then we reached North Beach. Golden sand curved beneath pastel houses like a postcard designed to lure fools. The IRONMAN swim arch stood proudly against the skyline, its red and black branding screaming overconfidence.

The harbour wall enclosed bobbing boats, beyond which lay the open sea—the same sea I would soon be swallowing by the pint. My stomach clenched, my heartbeat thundered in my ears.

Connie squeezed my hand. "You're very pale," she observed, ever the Florence Nightingale of sarcasm. "You should eat something."

IRONMAN Wales turns the Five Arches Car Park into what the organisers call Athlete Village and the rest of us call Stress in a car park. The place buzzed like a hive of bilingual panic. Signs and volunteers funnelled us inexorably toward registration.

The expo was a corridor of temptation masquerading as necessity. Merchandise stretched to the horizon: hoodies in the precise shade of You've Definitely Earned This, T-shirts listing every climb as though each were a cherished ex-lover, mugs declaring TENBY – IRON TOWN. There was even a rack of last year's kit—dangerous, discounted, whispering buy me and believe. Connie intercepted like a customs officer.
"One item," she decreed. "Something that isn't a bike."
I chose a hoodie, of course. Weakness is my super-power, and Tenby knows it.

Nutrition stands handed out shots of lurid liquid labelled Citrus Bang and Not Quite Lemon. I sampled one and discovered a new flavour: citrus, heartbreak and battery acid.

Another stall offered energy chews with names like Rocket Berry. Jack stole four, instantly declaring himself race-ready. Ellie filmed me chewing, captioned it Man vs. Jelly: The Struggle is Real, and uploaded before I'd swallowed.

The mechanic's tent resembled a triage ward for over-stressed machinery. Two saintly men in aprons moved from bike to bike with the calm of surgeons on sedatives. "Any creaks?" one asked, ear to a crankset.
"My soul," I nearly said, but offered the bike instead.
He spun the pedals, nodded, dabbed some oil, and gave me the indulgent smile of a GP humouring a hypochondriac. "You'll be fine." I clutched the phrase as if it were notarised.

A wetsuit vendor displayed rows of black neoprene optimism. Prospective customers writhed into samples like determined eels, while an assistant misted anti-fog spray into goggles with priestly reverence. Nearby, a stall I immediately christened Guardians of Chafe sold friction-sticks in travel size. Connie bought two and labelled them NECK and ARMPIT with a Sharpie, because marriage is 90 percent logistics and 10 percent damage control.

We arrived at the course-map wall: an enormous mural of my impending doom. The swim appeared as a tidy rectangle— soothing on paper, murderous in reality. The bike route wound around Pembrokeshire like tangled spaghetti; the run looped through Tenby four times, as if designed by a sadist with obsessive-compulsive tendencies. Groups of athletes clustered before it, nodding gravely like art critics pretending to understand cubism. A self-appointed expert with a laser pointer tapped a hill and announced, "Here's where your soul leaves your body." Everyone nodded thoughtfully, as though souls were optional extras.

Further along stood a Sharpie Station — for anyone keen to immortalise their poor judgement in permanent ink.

Old hands posed like Roman generals; first-timers practised finish-line faces and discovered that fear photographs poorly. A charity tent rattled buckets and distributed cowbells. Jack acquired one immediately and tested it every twelve seconds. Bella approved wholeheartedly.

At one table a bakery offered squares of Bara brith for Bravery. It tasted of reassurance and cinnamon. Opposite, a massage-tent sign-up sheet filled faster than the NHS. The final column read Post-Heartbreak Triage, which I suspected was not metaphorical.

The registration area itself was a bureaucratic miracle: rows of laptops, scanners, and volunteers so cheerful they could have organised D-Day with clipboards. Foam boards divided queues by surname; another barked Photo ID and Tri Licence Required. I patted pockets like a man defusing a bomb and produced my driving licence with the relief of a pilgrim finding water.

At the front sat a woman with a Pembrokeshire accent thick enough to butter toast. "Name, love?"
"Ian Dawson," I managed, throat dry.
She scanned my code, checked my ID, and, for one dreadful

second, I imagined her saying no record found. Instead she smiled, clicked something, and said, "Welcome to IRONMAN Wales, Ian. Here's your wristband."

She looped a thick white band around my wrist and snapped it shut with bureaucratic finality. "That doesn't come off till you finish," she chirped. "Cut it early and you're cut from the race."

The plastic tightened like a shackle. Around me hundreds of others wore the same mark. We had been tagged for re-release into the wild. There would be no quiet exit now, no pretending we'd merely come for the chips. I turned to Connie; she nodded—a look that mixed pride with impending widowhood.

The volunteer handed over a black backpack emblazoned with the IRONMAN dragon. "Everything you need's in there. Now go face the dragon!" she said with the alarming cheer of someone who isn't about to do so herself.

We took one last lap of the expo. Charity tents, club banners, children signing up for Iron Kids—a sort of gladiator preschool. Ellie made me pose under a banner reading FACE THE DRAGON while she filmed a slow zoom on my expression of dread. Connie squeezed my wristband again. "Right," she said, "you're official. Let's feed you before you start buying commemorative tea towels."

***

Back at the B&B I unpacked the bag like a man unearthing a time capsule of anxiety.

Inside: a bib number large enough to double as a sail, matching stickers for helmet and bike, a fluorescent swim cap the shade of radioactive custard, safety pins, and temporary number tattoos for both arms and calves—useful if my body parts become separated. The wristband glared at me accusingly. Beneath it all lay the timing chip: a small black rectangle on a velcro strap, the sporting equivalent of a parole tag.

Then came the bags themselves: blue for bike, red for run, white for street clothes, and the infamous pink drawstring sack—the Cinderella slipper of triathlon. The manual decreed: Place trainers inside; wear them for the run from swim exit to T1 up the zig-zag path. Failure to retrieve it promptly could mean disqualification. I pictured it fluttering unattended on the zig zags as officials shook their heads, while I sat sobbing in a penalty tent explaining that a seagull had made off with my race plan.

Finally, a glossy guidebook the thickness of a novella: course maps, cut-off times, infractions, and photographs of ecstatic finishers whose smiles had to be Photoshopped. The swim looked simple enough for a toddler's colouring book: two laps, with an awkward beach run between. The bike course, however, resembled the wiring diagram of an aircraft; its place-names read like a medieval poem—Wiseman's Bridge, Saundersfoot, Heartbreak Hill. The run looped through Tenby four times, which meant the crowd would witness my gradual decomposition in high definition.

The booklet cheerfully explained that spectators grow rowdier with each lap: lap one, polite applause; lap two, pints aloft; lap three, full choir; lap four, spontaneous karaoke and delusional encouragement. By the time I stagger through, someone in a dragon onesie will be insisting I'm winning.

The cut-off times glared at me: 2 hours 20 for the swim, 10 hours 30 for the bike, 17 overall. My best-case calculations ended with me crossing the line minutes before midnight, pursued by a man rolling up the carpet.

***

Tenby had transformed into a carnival of endorphins and unrealistic expectations.

Stalls continued to sell kit you never knew you needed — all bright and shiny, almost whispering your name. Carbon bottle cages "tested in a wind tunnel," anti-chafing balm infused with "confidence," and a £40 visor claiming to reduce negative thoughts. Even the towels were "triathlon-specific," as if drying off had an elite category. Aerodynamic helmets that could double as kitchen appliances, and shirts boasting I Beat the

Dragon—though buying one before racing felt like writing my own obituary.

We bribed the children with ice cream and wandered to the harbour to watch hardcore athlete's practise. Neon swim caps bobbed on the waves; others jogged up the zig-zag stairs to test their hamstrings and faith whilst I trudged beside them like a condemned cow touring the abattoir. Volunteers taped signs to lampposts, and locals leaned on railings with pints, pointing out future casualties. The air smelled of salt, chips, and destiny.

The sun slid behind the cliffs, cafés strung with fairy lights blinked awake, and my children abandoned triathlon entirely for the arcade claw machine. Connie leaned against me.
"You okay?" she asked.
I nodded, because lying is quicker than therapy. Inside, every organ had been replaced with a helium balloon and Tenby kept handing me pins.

***

Back at the B&B I unpacked my rucksack like a man disarming an emotional explosive. Every item was a reminder of choices made by someone who clearly needed adult supervision: one wetsuit that smelled faintly of despair, three nutrition bars modelled on drywall, and enough sticky gels to re-tile a bathroom. I spread them across the bed in perfect rows, the way generals arrange soldiers before sending them to certain death. Connie appeared in the doorway, arms folded, face set to domestic disappointment level two.

"Is this necessary?"

"It's called being thorough," I said, with the confidence of a man who'd just alphabetised his panic.

"It looks like anxiety with stationery."

She wasn't wrong. My colour-coded system looked less like preparation and more like a personality disorder having a rummage sale. The red bag for the run, the blue for the bike, the white for the post-mortem, and the pink for shame. Ellie poked her head in, took one look, and muttered, "He's nesting." Jack slapped a spare sticker on Bella's forehead and declared her the race marshal.

I taped my number onto the helmet with surgical precision, then retaped it for spiritual reassurance. The room smelt of neoprene and impending doom.

Connie re-entered with two mugs of tea, because in Britain every crisis, from a stubbed toe to a constitutional collapse, is accompanied by tea. "You've done everything," she said. "All that's left is to relax."

"Relax?" I said, as though she'd suggested nudity at a job interview. The word hovered in the air, ridiculous and obscene.

I perched on the bed and studied my wristband. It gleamed in the lamplight: a plastic circle of destiny, the friendship bracelet of the damned. "Don't cut it off," Connie said, reading my thoughts.

"I wasn't going to."

"You were."

She was right, of course. The thing felt like a GPS tag for idiots. "It's not a wristband," I said. "It's a contract — my ticket to the red carpet."

To re-assert dominance over my own nerves, I re-packed both transition bags for the eighth time. It achieved nothing except moving fear from one compartment to another, but at least it looked decisive. Satisfied, I tied them up, stacked them neatly by the door and admired them as a man might admire his own gallows.

We joined the conga line of athletes wheeling bikes into the Seafront Car Park. A volunteer with a scanner and the kindest eyes in Wales held out a hand. "Wristband, love." Beep. "Helmet on for me?" I clicked the strap; she tug-tested it like a school tie. "Two fingers under, tidy. Numbers on bike and helmet? Bar-end plugs in? Lovely. Rack down there by your number. See you tomorrow, butt."

Overnight the place had grown from car park to small city: numbered racks in military rows, arrows cable-tied to lampposts, mount/dismount lines chalked like crime scenes.

I wheeled the bike to my numbered slot—Row S, position 217—between a spaceship TT rig and a sensible dad-bike. I hung it by the saddle, hated the angle, re-hung it for better feng shui, then gave it a pat. "Sleep well, little friend," I said, like a man tucking in a racehorse.

We regrouped outside the barriers and walked Tenby at an easy dawdle, letting the town's noise slip past us.

Oddly, my stress was idling at 'polite concern,' while Connie's had revved to 'air-traffic control in a thunderstorm.' I'd developed the serene fatalism of a man who's already handed his fate to the sea; she'd developed a new superpower where she could spot an unlabelled bag from forty yards and worry it into compliance. "You're very calm," she said, which is British for Are you about to cry or combust? "Borrowed calm," I said. "Due back Monday."

Dinner was fish and chips—because no athlete in history has been fuelled by quinoa and lived happily. Connie was in full operational mode, cross-referencing tide times with cut-off charts and muttering in the tone of someone preparing for a small invasion. Her notebook had tabs. That's when I knew things were serious.

Ellie watched her with fascination. "Is Mum entering the race too, or just running logistics for NATO?"
Jack didn't look up from his chips. "She's doing both."

I chewed thoughtfully, mostly to avoid answering questions. Outside, laughter drifted through the open window, the kind that only comes from people who aren't racing.

Afterwards, we walked the Esplanade, the town caught in that strange half-light between anticipation and bedtime. Tenby gleamed—colourful shopfronts still open, music spilling from bars, and the faint hum of athletes pretending to be relaxed. The sea caught the lamplight like it was storing secrets. Down below, North Beach lay pristine and smug, its sand combed flat by machines that didn't know what was coming.

Families leaned on railings, kids licking ice creams the size of their heads. Volunteers unloaded barriers, dragging them across the tarmac with the sound of distant thunder. Every sign, every arrow, every fence was a reminder that tomorrow had been built for this — and somehow, so had I.

Connie slipped her arm through mine. "Ready?" she asked. "Almost," I said. "Just need to remember how to swim, bike, and run."
She laughed quietly. "You'll be fine."
Her voice didn't sound convinced, but somehow, it helped anyway.

Back in our room the air smelled of salt and carpet disinfectant. I arranged my shoes by the door—because civilisation collapses without neat footwear—and hung the wetsuit on the wardrobe like a damp omen. Connie inspected the scene, nodded, and said, "Acceptable." For her, that was practically a standing ovation.

Ellie brushed her teeth and announced she'd be filming the anthem "in case you cry like that bloke in the documentary." Jack asked again if the medal was chocolate. Bella sighed and pretended to die.

I set three alarms: Get Up, Get Up Now, and You've Ruined Everything. I rehearsed my morning routine aloud—porridge, wetsuit, pink bag, despair—like a Shakespearean soliloquy performed for household objects.

Connie switched off the light and took my hand. "You've done the hard bit," she said softly. "All the mornings. The wet towels. The rides in the rain. Tomorrow's just the bit everyone sees."

"That's the bit where I collapse," I said.

"Possibly," she smiled. "But collapse with style."

She kissed my forehead and turned out the light. Outside, Tenby murmured: a gull, a laugh, the sea breathing steadily like an experienced therapist. I stared into the dark as my mind staged a full-colour slideshow of disaster—waves, panic, punctures, blisters, public weeping. Somewhere between 'punctures' and 'weeping,' sleep finally tackled me from behind.

When I dreamt, I was halfway up Heartbreak Hill being pelted with leeks by a choir. My pink bag floated past like a smug jellyfish.

At four-thirty the alarm exploded. For a moment I thought the race had ended without me and felt oddly relieved. Then reality marched in.

The kitchenette looked like an abandoned prop cupboard. I created porridge of such density it might later be classified as a building material, drizzled honey over it for morale, and washed it down with coffee that tasted faintly of stress in liquid form.

Connie emerged wrapped in the B&B dressing gown like the ghost of sensible decisions. "You're up early," she said.

"I'm off to participate in recreational drowning," I replied.

She took a sip of my coffee, grimaced, and handed it back. "May the Lord have mercy."

Inventory time. Wetsuit: present, judgmental. Swim cap: shade of radioactive custard. Goggles: tiny transparent bullies. Pink bag: glowing in the corner, quietly plotting my humiliation.

I wriggled into the wetsuit to the hips—the international symbol for 'regret with commitment.' Getting it over the shoulders required more grunting than a farmyard. By the time the zip was up, I was both sweating and swearing internally in several languages.

"Need help?" Connie asked.

"I need a priest," I said.

She tugged the zip firmly, then stepped back to admire her handiwork. "Magnificent. Like a very determined sausage."

I could barely breathe. "If I collapse, tell the coroner I died fashionable."

"Final checklist?" she said.

"Bag, hat, goggles, rubber prison."

"Perfect," she smiled. "Go and be slightly heroic. We'll bring the shouting."

The children surfaced as I reached for the door. Ellie murmured, "Make it cinematic." Jack whispered, "Don't drown." Bella opened one eye, judged me comprehensively, and went back to sleep.

Outside, the corridor glowed with that guilty pre-dawn light that makes everything look like a confession. Somewhere down the street a gull laughed—a full, cackling laugh that sounded like it had seen my training logs.

I paused, drew a breath that didn't help, and muttered, "Alright, Tenby. Place your bets."

Then I set off down the corridor like a seal late for brunch, armed with nothing but a pink bag, wetsuit, and a bright yellow swim helmet—and the serene knowledge that I was about to spend an entire day proving, beyond reasonable doubt, that optimism is a diagnosable condition.

Chapter 24: The Swim of Slight Survival

I opened the B&B door and the air hit me—not festival buzz, but the hushed dread you get outside a dentist five minutes before the drill. Tenby had put on its big-event face and then pressed mute. The street felt like the corridor outside an exam hall: damp cobbles, lamps humming, everyone walking as if noise might void their warranty. Somewhere down the hill a wetsuit zip went riiiiip and every human on the peninsula heard it. A volunteer in hi-vis cupped a tea like a holy relic and spoke in library tones; even the gulls had ratcheted the menace down from "pirate" to "undertaker." Something enormous was about to happen, and we were all early and slightly underdressed for it. Doors opened, exhaled athletes, and shut again with the secrecy of confessionals.

I wore a hoodie and, yes, a bin-liner poncho—warmth and prophecy in one elegant crinkle. Fate, as ever, had a sense of humour and a bulk-buy account. Other figures emerged in identical rustle-wear, anonymous and shiny, a clandestine order of kitchen-sack knights shuffling towards transition to perform our final rituals. We nodded at each other like conspirators who had mislaid the plot.

"Morning," said a volunteer at the corner, smile tucked neatly round his words. Foam finger pointed toward the faint gold over North Beach. "You'll be grand."

"Grand" felt optimistic. "Marginally functional" would do nicely.

We joined the flow—athletes, families, prams containing toddlers in dinosaur onesies, and a labrador wearing a Welsh flag bandana with the gravitas of a regimental colonel. The air plaited together salt, coffee and Deep Heat into a scent best described as "determined." A café hatch glowed; a woman dispensed steaming cups to any hand not already occupied with a nervous habit. "On the house for athletes," she said. Proof that kindness cuts straight through caffeine and has fewer side effects.

Speakers crackled somewhere ahead—sound checks, a chord or two, a voice trying out its morning self: "Good morning, Tenby!" The crowd answered with a low ripple, like the beach had learned to purr.

We reached the sea front. North Beach lay below, a dark sheet lifting to a line of patient buoys—the ghostly punctuation of our imminent panic. Floodlights lacquered the sand with theatrical gold. Volunteers lined the path, their breath making small clouds, their hands perpetually, helpfully pointing. Cowbells clanked in the distance. Somewhere a laugh escaped and was promptly swallowed by the scale of it all.

"Pink-bag pegs down there," a marshal said, reading my shamefully hot-pink accessory like tea leaves. "Don't forget to collect it at on the way up" he added, with the earnest repetition of a man who'd seen things.

"Don't forget to collect it at on the way up," I repeated—my new devotional chant.

I followed a breadcrumb trail of pink towards the zig-zag railings now sprouting fluorescent drawstring fruit. A volunteer clocked my number. "Tidy. Pop it there—number facing out. Lovely job."

I hung the bag like a coat in a very judgmental cloakroom and breathed in—completely useless, but it felt procedural.

"If I forget it?" I asked, because I know myself.

"You won't," she smiled. "And if you try, fifty strangers will shout your number until you remember. This is Tenby."

Quite.

As I touched base with Connie, we watched the beach compose itself. Self-seeded boards went up like hedgerow signposts—expected swim times: under 1:00, 1:10, 1:20, 1:30... Athletes drifted into shoals beneath each number. The sub-1:00 pen looked improbably serene, the way surgeons look serene before re-arranging organs; my pen looked like a book club that had accidentally joined the Marines.

Ellie arrived with Jack, phone already filming. She panned along the boards with the reverence of a nature documentary. "Here we observe the middle-aged male in his flimsy bin-liner plumage, attempting to appear brave."

Jack tugged my wetsuit sleeve. "Dad, Ellie says you're going to DNF. What's that?"

"DNF?" I said, with the bright confidence of a man lying to a customs officer. "Dad Never Fails. Trademark pending."

"It means Did Not Finish," Ellie replied, not looking up. "He made that up."

Jack considered this and nodded. "I prefer Dad's."

"Excellent taste," I said. "We'll go with the deluxe version."

The announcer's voice rose and fell—useful timings, a reminder about the swim-exit funnel, jokes calibrated to reduce the urge to flee. Then the music changed key; the crowd shifted with it; a group moved to the sea's edge with the quiet marching-band gravity that tells your bones what's next.

The anthem.

You can hear it on YouTube and social media, but there's something about a thousand people going still on a Welsh morning that makes your heart stand to attention even if your knees won't. The beach stilled, and the first note rose; then all of us with it. I'm Welsh; the words live somewhere behind my ribs, but today they felt newly minted. I sang, and for a minute everything lined up like a well-oiled chain.

Even the kayakers laid paddles across laps like folded arms in chapel. I knew every syllable from school halls and rugby Saturdays, but here, shoulder to shoulder, it put steady ground beneath feet that had been vibrating like tuning forks since dawn. Halfway through, I stopped thinking about the sea, the zig-zags, Wiseman's Bridge, the clock, the pink bag, my questionable will. The nerves finally took their seats and agreed to behave. When the last phrase settled, nobody rushed the silence. We let it stand. We meant it.

When sound returned, the beach exhaled as one.

Bin-liner off. The morning nipped at my arms. Wetsuit already on — I did the universal neoprene shoulder-shimmy (the motion we all pretend is dignified) just to settle it. Bodyglide had earned its pension; no stuck seams, no gossip. A fellow athlete checked my zip with the tenderness one reserves for cellos. Goggles perched on forehead, cap in hand, timing chip checked with the fervour of a pilgrim—left ankle, faithful, present. A volunteer proffered a dollop of Vaseline with the solemnity of a communion wafer. I dabbed, nodded, and attempted the face of a man who always knows exactly where to put petroleum jelly at dawn.

I stepped into my pen. Conversation had drained away. We'd spent our jokes; all that remained was the breath, the shuffle and the tiny private ceremonies—a tap on a watch, a kiss to a ring, a quick forehead-to-fist prayer. We were queueing for something equally holy and ridiculous.

The announcer's voice softened, as though reading a bedtime story to people who'd chosen a very peculiar nap. "Here we go then, Tenby. Lovely day to be brave." Watches beeped in timid harmony. Caps pulled down. Goggles pressed. Even the shore seemed to hold its lungs.

"Ten..." Our line crept. "Five... four... three... two... one—" The klaxon split the morning clean in two. The beach exploded into motion: thousands of feet slapping the sand, and me amongst them, arms somewhere between windmill and semaphore. Dignity optional, belief compulsory.

My heart attempted escape via my throat; I patted it back like a skittish terrier.

From B&B doorway to this exact grain of sand, I'd been collecting permissions—the volunteer's "You'll be grand," the café's charity brew, the anthem like a laid-down path, Connie's squeeze of a hand. Even the bin-liner had been a benediction: if I could dress as refuse and still walk toward the sea, I could probably survive whatever came next.

I closed my eyes for one beat and thought of the idiotic click that started this—bin-liners I never bought, months of wobbling and wheezing and returning, the glorious Welsh wave of encouragement that both slices and stitches you simultaneously.

"Not today, fear," I said, quietly enough that only the sea could eavesdrop.

Cap down. Goggles on. Marshal's hand flicked—there, now—and I stepped with everyone else, into the morning that would decide the rest of the day.

The line fed us toward the water, and then suddenly there was no sand left to argue with. Spreadsheets, pool drills, open-water panics rehearsed in smaller ponds—useful, yes, but you can't truly prepare a person who regularly forgets why he went upstairs for four minutes for a 3.8-kilometre conversation with the Atlantic.

The first ankle-deep slap was invigorating; the second rose to committee level; by knee-depth the sea had convened a tribunal. The dive—awkward, protective of goggles, more surrender than swan—switched the world to cold and noise. A clamp took my chest. Face numb. Breath a stubborn stranger. And the taste—good grief—the taste. Not the pure salt of heroic narratives, but salt with a tang of diesel, as if Poseidon had been tinkering with a lawnmower. A safety boat must have idled near; my mouth burned like a cross word. I resisted the urge to retch, kept my head up until the palate shifted from "shipyard mishap" to "brine with a grievance," and then went face-down into the business of it.

Tenby, viewed underwater, refuses glamour. Not green, not clear, more "old bottle glass someone's breathed on." I just about saw my hands, caught a flicker of a calf, and then met the locals: jellyfish. Dozens of translucent saucers drifting like distracted duchesses. One patted my chin. I made a noise audible only to bubbles and carried on.

Within seconds of pretending to find a stroke, I was kicked in the face. Not malicious, merely the standard greeting of mass starts. A heel glanced my goggle; water sloshed in; my right eye became the North Sea. I stopped, treaded water in the thundering melee, reseated the goggle while a forest of limbs churned past, collected a polite elbow to the ear and a stranger's hand to the thigh. It's remarkable how swiftly you resign yourself to intimate contact with strangers when the alternative is sinking like a wet biscuit.

On paper, IRONMAN Wales offers a child's rectangle: out, across, back, beach, repeat. In practice, it's a washing machine stuffed with otters and the occasional soup spoon. Once my face thawed and breathing downgraded from mutiny to heavy sarcasm, I found a rhythm: pull, roll, breathe; pull, roll, breathe. The first leg outward felt like a kilometre or ten, each stroke prising me from land. Cheeks stung; core warmed; fingers prickled as blood returned like angry wasps. The diesel ghost receded. Salt took up residence. You can drink all day and remain heroically thirsty.

Sighting proved comic. Sun rising behind the harbour, glare turning the sea into a field of broken mirrors. The yellow buoys, so cheerfully near on land, transformed into deceitful tricksters. Sight—swim for what felt like a paragraph—sight again— discover the buoy had not, in fact, budged. Distance at sea is a pathological liar. My left goggle fogged, gifting me a monocle view of chaos. I tried to time breaths with wave tops and not inhale froth like a cappuccino. A kayak slid near. "You're heading for Ireland, love—turn left!" came the Pembrokeshire instruction, slicing through panic with the efficiency of a bread knife. Another marshal leant toward a swimmer clutching his bow. "You're on time, butt. Float a tick, then off you go." Calm voices as temporary scaffolding.

What do you think about for two kilometres out to sea? Everything and its opposite. My brain split itself into departments. One counted strokes. One watched the breath. One delivered a rolling newsfeed of useful nonsense. Two... three... breathe left. Still salty. Diesel gone. Jellyfish? No—

stringy seaweed. Breathe right. Can I see the buoy? Don't drift. He said left. LEFT. A song fragment insisted on looping: You've got a friend in me, which felt sarcastic given my current relationship status with the ocean. I wondered what Connie was doing—probably scanning the waterline for my impression of a distressed otter. Imagined Ellie capturing my ferret-in-a-flood face for her followers; pictured Jack composing questions about sharks and snacks. Thought of Him—my private rival with the buoyant moustache, somewhere out here slicing the water like a buttered eel while I paddled like someone trapped in a duvet cover. Then thought about bin-liners, bacon, my pillow, whether jellyfish possess teeth, and whether I'd locked the car. All noble strategies to avoid noticing my arms were filing formal grievances.

Incidents occurred. A slimy ribbon looped my hand—panic, flail, oh good, seaweed. A plastic bag attempted to marry my face; my brain yelled "Jellyfish!"; reason strolled in three strokes later to peel it away. Once I followed a trail of bubbles like a trusting duckling, only to discover the owner had stopped to adjust goggles and I nearly head-butted his hope. Repeatedly, a wayward kick thudded the back of my head, like being tapped by an impatient librarian. You curse internally, you adjust, you persist. Ego has no place here; there's only etiquette and survival.

At last the first buoy arrived properly, not as a mirage—yellow planet bobbing with the self-importance of a department head. Rounding it felt like turning a corner in a hedge maze. Swing left, sight the next, and immediately discover the cross-leg was bumpier—a current had decided to hold a staff meeting. Arms, now thoroughly warmed and muttering, kept time. I slid past a gentleman in a moustache doing breaststroke with conversational ease, head high, expression benign. "Morning," he said, as if we were passing in a tearoom. Freddy. Of course. My personal nemesis, serenely gossiping with the ocean while I auditioned for the role of Drowning Hedgehog. A small, childish spark ignited. I lowered my head and bought an extra tablespoon of effort. Salt bit. The point, minor but delicious, was made.

The shore re-appeared like a bribe. In the shallows the world sharpened; sand rippled beneath like combed hair, shells winking. The taste changed again—still salt, now with undertones of humus and reheated seaweed—a flavour one might call "nostalgic harbour." Fingers scuffed bottom. Time to stand.

Legs, on loan from a newborn giraffe, attempted duty. I rose, sat, rose again; the wave tugged like a clingy relative. I argued, wobbled, and won on points.

There is nothing dignified about the Australian exit. Hundreds of wetsuited creatures erupting from the sea like a low-budget mythology, jogging thirty metres across cold sand only to fling themselves back in for another serving. It's absurd and, therefore, perfect. I trotted the beach; calves howled; and there were my people on the railings—Ellie filming with grim delight, Jack waving a sign that read GO DAD! (Ice Cream?) with priorities perfectly aligned, Connie clapping like morale in human form, Bella barking with the authority of a harbourmaster. My heart attempted a cartwheel. I offered a thumb-up that looked suspiciously like a hooked claw. A volunteer thrust a cup; I sipped the sweetest, plastickiest water known to man. A teenager in a dragon onesie hammered a cowbell with operatic zeal. A volunteer dressed as a leek cried, "GOGGLES DOWN, BUTT! YOU'LL GO FASTER!"—which, frankly, is the sort of coaching I respond to.

Re-entering after that little beach run hurt more than the first plunge. Blood had dallied in my legs; the ocean took offence and reapplied the chill with interest. Arms ached; shoulders had adopted the tone of a disappointed headmaster; and the thought of doing The Rectangle again felt like being told to climb back up a mountain you've just come down to fetch the picnic you forgot. There was no door marked EXIT. I dove. Diesel's ghost kissed my lips, then salt, then the familiar cocktail of neoprene and panic management. The mind piped up: Why are we here again? Haven't we demonstrated enough pluck for one morning? I invited it to hush. One more lap. One buoy at a time.

The field had loosened its corset; there was room to be distinctly mediocre without being trampled. I found temporary colleagues: a cap whose cadence matched mine for a few hundred metres; a pair of feet producing bubbles I gratefully drafted behind until they veered off to pursue their own novel life choices. Karma matters—when I accidentally tapped an ankle I apologised into my bubbles as if the ocean could pass along the message.

Halfway to the far buoy, a man leaned on a kayak in contemplation. The marshal murmured steadiness; the man nodded, rejoined. Seeing someone decide not to quit sits nicely in the lungs. It reminded me of those early lake days—flipping on my back, staring at sky, making a bargain with breath. I kept pulling.

Round the final buoy and homeward—the sound from land travelled across the water like a rumour: cowbells, horns, a choir of human optimism. The railings had filled, Tenby settling in for its favourite pastime—cheering total strangers. The thought presented itself: you might actually finish this swim. My hand kissed sand. Up. Legs? Present. Cooperative-ish. I lurched into gravity like a first date.

The pink-bag railings hove into view and, like a kindly lighthouse, there was my number. My fingers, now resembling cold vegetable peelers, wrestled the drawstring. A volunteer reached to help; my pride performed a fussy little ballet and did it myself. Trainers on over sandy feet—like stuffing squid into jam jars. And then the famous kilometre of stair-flavoured jogging.

"Run" is perhaps ambitious. I tottered up the zig-zags, flanked by barriers and Tenby's incomparable chorus. Spectators leaned in with their unique blend of affection and gentle insult. A man in a daffodil hat boomed, "MY NAN FLOATS FASTER!" A woman brandishing a Welsh flag shouted, "COME ON MY LOVERS, UP YOU GO!" Children rattled cowbells like overcaffeinated toddlers at a percussion lesson. An elderly lady, tea in hand, said, very softly, "Well done, my love." And that nearly undid me. Halfway up, a calf clenched like a tiny fist. I yelped in my soul. A volunteer jogged alongside, hand to my elbow. "Keep moving, it'll let go," he said, and it did, sulking.

We passed the fire station; passed guesthouse windows framing curious heads with hair like startled hay; passed a gentleman in a bathrobe clapping one-handed and offering a dignified "Da iawn!" to everyone equally. The pink bag had earned its keep. My toes were sandy but not sacrificial.

And then the car park—rows of bikes gleaming like mechanical cavalry—daunting, comforting, absurdly beautiful. The worst bit, for me, was behind. T1 would now provide both chaos and sanctuary.

Transition resembled the aftermath of a polite neoprene tornado. Racks upon racks of bikes hung by saddles like sleeping bats. Blue and red bags queued in orderly rows. Volunteers pointed, beckoned, ushered—the air-traffic controllers of human bad ideas. The smell had pivoted: less ocean, more chain lube, rubber and anxiety sugar.

I attacked the wetsuit as one wrestles an eel with boundaries. Hands shook. Fingers had become decorative items. For a brief, doomed moment I considered cycling in it and submitting to maritime law. At last—schlupp—the suit surrendered. Sand was discovered in locations not listed in any brochure. I wiped my face with a towel and achieved a pleasing paste of grit. Cap off; a litre of sea fell down my torso with comedic determination.

Autopilot, but British farce. Bike top on—zip fussed like a dowager. Socks over pruned feet with all the grace of upholstering a hedgehog. Shoes—wooden little prisons after all that compliant water. Helmet on. Sunglasses—because if you can't be fast, you can at least be slightly theatrical. Race belt secured. A volunteer called, "Chip on left ankle? Helmet clipped? Lovely—off you go!" I tapped the timing chip as a footballer taps the stadium sign, because ritual is nourishment.

I lifted my bike from the rack. Somewhere, a marshal yelled, "Dai the Postie's gone up Wiseman's twice already!" Of course he had. In Tenby folklore, even the postal service climbs better than you.

I jogged to the mount line on legs that had congealed into blancmange and, as I clipped one foot in, allowed myself a single, luxurious thought about the past ninety minutes: I had swum 3.8 kilometres in a petulant ocean, sampled diesel à la mode, tasted kelp, taken a slap from a plastic bag, been repeatedly tenderised by strangers' ankles, and briefly hunted my moustachioed figment across a rectangle. I'd run up a cliff in neoprene while an enthusiastic leek shouted technical advice. I was wet, cold, sandy, mildly indignant—and, against reason, quietly delighted.

The part I'd dreaded most had not defeated me.

Which, in Tenby, is the beginning of all sorts of trouble.

Chapter 25: Bike. Pain. Repeat

This was the portion I'd dreaded almost as much as the aquatic mugging. The IRONMAN Wales bike leg is not a pastoral pootle past docile sheep and forgiving tea shops. It's a stern letter from geography, written on the stationery of narrow lanes and stapled to your quads with 18% gradients. Veterans all delivered the same counsel with the benevolent smile of those who've already been to the gallows: pace yourself now or the second lap will arrive with a handbag and wallop you. And eat—because misjudge the nutrition and the marathon will treat you like unclaimed luggage.

We funnelled through Tenby's narrow streets to a corridor of rampant good will. Residents, families, and absolute strangers leaned over barriers, ringing cowbells and waving flags as if summoning us from the underworld. A man in a full dragon suit bellowed, "GO ON! EASY UP, HARD DOWN!" with the intimacy of an old friend and the lung capacity of a pipe organ. Children offered high fives; I managed a grazing contact that likely ranked as a low-speed collision. The town walls lifted from the morning light like documentary evidence that I had, in fact, just negotiated the sea. The day was cool, sun coyly low, with rumours of wind later. I tucked into the drops and attempted a relationship with rhythm.

Pastel houses gave way to rolling fields, drystone and sheep regarding us with the hauteur of aristocrats wondering why their drive was full of Lycra. Easy gear, soft cadence. My quads were unimpressed by the job reallocation from swimming to pedalling; a fresh department filed a grievance. Shoulders down. Breathe like a grown-up. A gel wrapper—gaffer-taped to my bars in training and now flapping like a critical aunt—reminded me to eat. Not yet, said the stomach. Settle first. For once, I obeyed.

A few miles later, the road flirted with a dip just as a crosswind arrived to collect its rent. Hedges parted, exposure yawned, and a sideways slap introduced the Pembrokeshire breeze as a character with poor boundaries. I leaned into it, recalling every fireside warning about gusts that could relocate a medium-sized cyclist to a different postcode. Left of me, a rider wobbled; another overcorrected and kissed my front wheel with his shadow. "Steady!" came a call—half counsel, half cautionary hymn. This was no broad-shouldered boulevard. This was rural Wales: lanes as thin as string and tarmac like emery board, eager to acquaint itself with your skin.

The course is a novel in three acts: one long westward swoop and two northern loops. The "long one" escorts you from Tenby past villages and cliff edges, winds you by Angle's rugged punctuation, then ushers you back. After that, you hang a turn onto a loop that climbs and drops like a caffeinated yo-yo—twice. Coachly literature calls it one of the world's nastier IRONMAN bikes. They are right. The climbs arrive like bills in January; the descents are narrow, technical, and allergic to complacency; the flats, when they exist, are largely rumours. Hammer early and the second lap will write you a letter beginning "Dearest Fool."

The road contracted to a suggestion as we threaded hedgerows and cottages. Farmers turned out in wellies to appraise the spectacle; a cow looked up, found us wanting, and returned to cud with theatrical boredom. Marshals in red, flags aloft, orchestrated the Lycra conga through junctions like benevolent traffic saints. A boy banged a saucepan with a spoon and chanted, "Faster! Faster!" while we trundled at a somewhat legal twelve miles per hour. A visionary.

I negotiated a banana as the road momentarily remembered kindness. The first feed station loomed—part refuelling depot, part morale spa. Also, crucially, the only respectable places to address plumbing. I had in training attempted the mid-ride trisuit unzip, a solo round of anatomical Twister conducted while moving, and vowed never again. At the station, volunteers presented bottles and snacks like Olympic torches. "Water! Isotonic! Banana! Bar!" each call a promise and a dare. I slowed, met a woman's eye, took water, and was awarded an approving, "Nice and easy. Don't try anything new!" Lovely to be understood so completely by a stranger.

For a sweet handful of miles the world behaved. Hedgerow, stone wall, a flirtatious flash of sea; a friendly tailwind appointed us all honorary cyclists. Then the road remembered it lived inland. The rises arrived in polite little rehearsals for the operas to come—nothing severe, merely reminders that this course doesn't believe in free lunches. I snacked as the minutes passed—bars in civilised bites, banana with the delicacy of a surgeon—and kept a suspicious eye on the potholes. Lamphey materialised with another feed station as if conjured by wishful thinking. Bottles refilled, a gel secured, and a marshal's cheerful "Keep it steady to Narberth!" tucked behind my ear like a hymn.

Lamphey to Narberth is a labyrinth laid by a bored cartographer. Narrow lanes squeezed by hedgerows, tarmac ribbed like corrugated iron, every slight down followed by a marginally less slight up. No generosity. The villages slipped by—Carew with its castle and spectators offering jelly babies like benedictions— and then the hills turned verbose. Long, grinding climbs unfurled through dim woodland that smelled of pine and damp earth. Someone had chalked "PACE YOURSELF OR PAY LATER" across the road with the jaunty menace of a Victorian quack. I laughed, then immediately coughed, having inhaled a jelly baby sideways. Narberth itself arrived with brass band bravado; locals cheered as if we'd all forgotten to tell them this wasn't the finish. My watch, however, was brutally literate: not halfway.

Coastward again, and a sign for Wiseman's Bridge (2 miles) caused my stomach to reposition itself. Tales of the 18% ramp had circulated like Gothic fiction. The village itself is a blink with a pub; the climb beyond is a treatise on gravity. I stood and ground—dignity optional, forward motion nominal—lungs staging a small opera, quads making the sound of hot metal. Spectators yelled in Welsh and English and whatever language is spoken by people waving inflatable hammers. The crest presented itself like an apology. Reward: a technical descent into Saundersfoot, one of the course's livelier theatres. Noise.

Bells. AC/DC from windows. Locals distributing high fives like communion. A left turn, a cheeky kicker—because why not— then the preamble to the infamous.

Heartbreak Hill. The gradient is not the most terminal, but the vibe is medieval tournament meets carnival. The road narrows to a human corridor; houses lean in; faces crowd the edges; your name is chanted if visible, invented if not. Palms slap. Horns bleat. Pots and pans aspire to symphony. A rugby fan briefly paced my wheel, yelling, "ONLY ONE MORE LAP!" with wicked optimism. The atmosphere defied physiology. At the top, a marshal rang a cowbell as if he depended on it for heat and bellowed, "Spin it out, boy!" I crested, bent, half laughing, half crying. Heartbreak: once kissed. To be revisited.

Post-Saundersfoot, the route sauntered back towards Tenby through St Brides Hill, which felt like a cool-down whisper after a gospel choir. Ladies in Welsh costume served tea and bara brith to spectators with the unflappable calm of officiants; a man in hi-vis mowed his lawn in studied indifference to the circus. The outskirts of Tenby brushed our wheels before the course sent us north onto the loop of repeats. The miles clicked: fifty, sixty, sixty-five. Gel in, sip, salt tab, scold stomach, repeat the apology. Eat every twenty minutes whether you feel like a picnic or a fainting Victorian. Drink even when you suspect you are made of water. Pee in civilisation, for the hedges are innocent and the marshals unforgiving.

At mile seventy-two, biology raised its hand. I held court until Narberth's station, dismounted with domesticated urgency, performed the portaloo ballet (wrestling a damp trisuit zip with the grace of a man fighting a squirrel), then remounted within two minutes—my quads objecting like tenants whose deposit has not been returned. They could sue later.

That second Narberth feed looked like a minor skirmish. Bottles rolled like marbles, bananas lay heroically crushed, volunteers flitted with jugs, one athlete slumped in a chair auditioning for Greek tragedy while marshals talked him back to mortal life with cups and kindness. I swapped empties for full, smiled in the style of a damp gargoyle. "Steady now," said a woman in that tender Pembrokeshire cadence. "Halfway gone. Save some for the run." The notion of running a marathon later felt sarcastic, like scheduling a piano recital after arm-wrestling a bear.

Back into the loop we went—Narberth, Wiseman's, Saundersfoot: the triad of woe—now under a ruffled afternoon sky. The breeze had developed opinions; headwind here, crosswind there, always unhelpful. The crowds had multiplied and fortified themselves on stout and pastry, which did wonders for the decibels. The first lap glowed dully in my legs. This is where the race bares its teeth. The second lap decides whether you will finish comfortably mortal or as a ghost.

Narberth's band now favoured pop classics. I swear "Sweet Caroline" tried to hug me. A woman whose sign earlier read "Smile if you're wearing Lycra" now held "You Paid For This!" I grinned at the indictment. Mental arithmetic simplified to the only rhythm that mattered: hill → gel → drink → descent → hill. I recalculated potential finish times with the diligence of a bookie. Wondered whether my family had had lunch. Pictured them in Saundersfoot, distributing chips and encouragement with equal generosity to strangers. Briefly resented them for this cheery treachery, then apologised to my bike for having such uncharitable thoughts. The bike forgave me. It had no choice.

Winding back toward Wiseman's, the gradient felt like it had acquired a grievance. Lower back tight, hands tender from bar-gripping, shoulders hunching like a guilty plot. I forced the grip to loosen and shook out the arms. At the crest, I reached for electrolytes and discovered the cage contained a philosophical emptiness. I had forgotten to refill. Splendid. A small sip of plain water, an attempt to fool the brain into imagining citrus—no sale—and a salt tab to appease the gods. My stomach, now a committee, passed a motion of no confidence.

On the drop to Saundersfoot, I overtook a rider who was weaving with the unsettling grace of seaweed. "Sorry—dizzy," he said as I edged past. "Drink! Eat! Gentle on the descent!" I called. He nodded and eased the brakes. An ambulance idled midway down, paramedics watching with that precise calm that says: yes, fun, but also physics. A moral postcard.

Saundersfoot had only grown wilder. AC/DC's "Highway to Hell" thundered across brick and beach as if auditioning to be the town anthem. The dragon-costumed herald had migrated to the base of the climb, banging a drum and yelling, "SAME AGAIN, BUTT! SAME AGAIN!" I pulled a face at him that suggested both affection and despair, then turned onto Heartbreak for the second courtship.

It hurt. Of course it did. The slope started steeper, the road narrowed to a funnel, and the noise... The noise telescoped until you could feel it on your teeth. Names pelted my ears. "IAN! IAN! HUP HUP HUP!" Painted dragons on small faces waved flags with violent sincerity. Elderly ladies clutched tea and dispensed "You're doing great!" with the absolute authority of grandmothers. An Elvis gyrated perilously near my bars. The rules of traffic no longer applied; you are simply willed upward by a crowd that refuses to let you disgrace the street. I watched my own legs in mild awe as they continued to turn of their own accord. Crest. Breath ragged. Heart pounding like borrowed timpani. Eyes prickling. Worth it.

The final miles back to Tenby blurred: hedges, potholes, a mist of rain, the ever-thickening chorus. Children waved name placards; lads in rugby shirts pioneered interpretive dancing; a woman on a mobility scooter rang a cowbell between her knees with devastating accuracy. Nearing town, a marshal's voice cut through: "Keep it steady into T2! Feet off before the line!" I glanced at my watch. A faintly embarrassing seven hours and change. But upright. Within cut-off. Containing enough hope to be dangerous.

The painted DISMOUNT band arrived like a truce. "Dismount! Dismount!" the volunteers sang. I swung a leg, unclipped, and met the ground on legs that had, quite frankly, had enough. The bike suddenly resembled a superior walking stick. A marshal caught my elbow with professional kindness. "Well done! Bike done!" Words so beautiful I nearly framed them.

I rolled into transition past serried ranks of already-sleeping bicycles. Cleats ticked on tarmac like a popcorn machine. T2 carried a different weather—quieter, drier, vaguely ecclesiastical. I located my red run bag, sat on the bench, and began the ceremony.

My red run bag delivered exactly what the guide had promised and precisely what my soul did not: a pair of aggressively dry socks and my "marshmallows for the feet," which immediately revealed themselves to be marshmallows forged by a small, vengeful god. I sat on a plastic bench, considered my toes—pruned, sandy, and drafting a grievance—and addressed them as if they were a fragile select committee. "It's just a marathon, boys. You behave, I'll behave." They remained in camera.

***

Race belt spun to announce me to the world from the front rather than the back. Cap donned to negotiate the rain and the hair situation. A careful swig of water without becoming a camel. Gels tucked into belt pouches with the tidy malice of concealed weapons. Legs: concrete with heritage status. Stomach: alternating between "Feed me" and "How dare you." Dignity: on a smoke break.

Around me, other pilgrims performed variations on the theme. One man executed a full costume change with the cheerful modesty of a festival-goer; another stared at the floor for sixty long seconds before standing as if he'd been wound with a key. Freddy's bike blinked in its rack without its owner. His running shoes had gone. Excellent. A target is healthful.

I stood—and paused. Transition had that peculiar hush of backstage five minutes before curtain. Bikes hung like sleeping bats, bags murmured in the breeze, marshals spoke as if in a chapel. Beyond the fencing, Tenby roared on—bells, cheers, a rhythm of feet. The rain slackened, the cloud clung. Two-thirds of a questionable dream were complete. Twenty-six miles and a handful of dignity separated me from a line and a medal that may or may not be chocolate. Body: mutinous. Mind: offering unprintable commentary. Heart: whispering, "You have come this far. One more act."

I clapped my hands to coax blood into numb fingers and said, audibly, "Right then. Let's go for a run." A volunteer smiled as if I'd told the correct answer. "You'll be grand, love," she said. "Don't forget to enjoy the crowd."

And so I jogged toward the exit—legs wooden, smile experimental—ready to exchange the tyranny of hills for the tyranny of laps. Somewhere ahead, Freddy's socks were already diminishing into the distance. Tenby's streets waited like a trap laid by optimism. My posterior objected; my back penned a sonnet of complaint; my pride had been sanded by potholes and AC/DC. But I was still in motion.

Bike faced. Pain endured. Now: repeat—this time on feet.

Chapter 26: Run, Ian, Run (Walk, Cry, Jog, Repeat)

I stumbled out of T2 like a foal attempting pointe work. Tenby's seafront car park had become a cross between a car boot sale and a field hospital: wetsuits peeled off with the sound of industrial tape, tri-suits were wrung as if they'd wronged someone personally, cramped calves were kneaded with the urgency of pastry in a thunderstorm, and shoes were being accused—loudly—of betrayal. Volunteers, those saints in hi-vis, barked crisp directions, dealt flat cola and banana slices with NHS-grade kindness, and managed somehow to look delighted about the whole circus.

On paper, the IRONMAN Wales marathon is four laps of ~10.5 km. In practice, it's an emotional theme park dressed as municipal roadwork. You exit along South Cliff Street, flirt with the town wall on South Parade, then trudge up Narberth Road to New Hedges where lap bands—elastic proof of suffering—are bestowed. You then slalom back through Tenby via the Croft and the harbour, duck under The Paragon arch, and take tea with the wind on the Esplanade. At the end of each lap the finish line winks, and a marshal kindly diverts you right onto Picton Terrace to repeat the joke. Only when your wrist jingles with four bands may you proceed straight with the smugness of the entitled.

The athlete guide purrs this like soothing GPS. Reality prefers the tone of a headmaster with a bell. Two minutes into South Cliff Street, both quads filed cease-and-desists. My shoulders, having stockpiled all the bike's tension like Victorian misers hoarding shillings, crept up round my ears. My stomach—fresh from a day of gels, salt and mid-bike citrus fireworks—called a vote of no confidence. A discreet burp offered tasting notes of banana, diesel and faint humiliation. Marvelous. We were making memories.

Within two hundred metres I discovered that running after 180 km on a bicycle is like asking an escalator to reverse for you because you said please. The body lunged, the feet slapped, and the mind detached, hovering above, making observational notes. Out of the corner of my eye—of course—Freddy. Moustache: damp, immaculate, and extremely pleased with itself. Compression socks: theatrical snowdrift. He trotted past, all breezy benevolence. "Still alive?" he chirped.

"Define alive," I wheezed. He chuckled and vanished, like an advert for smugness.

The road tilted in that Welsh way—apparently flat, morally uphill. Toddlers with sticky hands demanded high fives; teenagers assaulted cowbells; men with pints leaned over railings to assure us it was "all downhill after New Hedges." It was not. The air smelled of salt, vinegar, and someone over-generous with the Deep Heat. If you haven't been cheered uphill by lightly soused locals while resembling an inflatable mattress losing an argument, do broaden your horizons.

Then my lot arrived, materialising like a support crew and public humiliation rolled into one. Dan, Baz and Kev wedged themselves behind the rail with a banner that read: DON'T BE SH$£ DON'T SH*% YOURSELF (tasteful redactions implied). Dan gave me a thumbs-up so dry it required irrigation. "Bold choice starting your marathon on legs." Baz shook a picnic hamper like a maraca. "No outside assistance," he announced piously, "so I'll selflessly eat this sausage roll for you." Kev cupped a megaphone like a man who once coached under-9s without permission. "CADENCE!" he bellowed, then leaned in, whispering, "That's a running thing, right?"
I grinned despite myself. It's hard to wilt while being heckled by your own pit crew.

Aid station one, roughly 1.5 miles in, was a village fête run by triathletes in fancy dress. A dragon thrust a gel. A leek proffered salted potato and small squares of science. A green-haired herald cried, "Water or cola!" with the urgency of a hostage negotiator. I chose cola. It fizzed down like a small party popper in my torso, and morale sat up straighter.

Leaving, I found myself beside an older gentleman from Birmingham wearing the expression of someone who has met eternity and found it poorly lit. "First IRONMAN," he gasped. "Does it get better?" Conscience and mischief fought; mischief landed the cleaner punch. "Oh yes," I said. "The hallucinations are delightful." He laughed, then inspected my face for sincerity. We both found none.

Narberth Road is deceptively simple on a map—a tidy line gently rising. Underfoot it's a series of false flats and earnest drags, with cambers designed by a committee of ankles' enemies. Hedgerows leaned in like nosy aunties, occasionally parting to reveal sheep administering silent judgment.

The field stretched into a procession of private treaties. Some walked with the serene pragmatism of future finishers; others maintained a stately shuffle. I adopted a pact: run to the next lamp post, walk thirty seconds, renew vows. My Garmin beeped every mile with the tyranny of a cheerful metronome. To distract myself, I conducted a sensory audit: tongue—lemon gel and road grit; nose—grass, sunscreen, a tease of diesel; ears— breath, footfalls, bells, the gentle Welsh art of affectionate abuse. Sometimes a whoop arose as someone spied their person and remembered why they'd volunteered for this farce.

Around mile three, New Hedges presented itself with gazebos and municipal glamour. Signs proliferated. "Tap here for power," said one, with a large red circle. I tapped and shouted, "Refund!"—pleasing the crowd if not the physics. Another promised, "Kiss me if you're desperate!" I weighed the optics and jogged on.

Volunteers at the band station held out elastic with coronation gravitas. "First band!" a lad declared. I slid it on. It looked ridiculous and felt holy. A friend had warned the first band makes you too sprightly. My heart rate, like a stern aunt, forbade sprightliness.

New Hedges squats near St Bride's Hill—Heartbreak on the bike course. Even on foot, its racket bled over: saucepan lids beaten to within an inch of their lives, calls of "Don't let the dragon catch you!" I promised not to. Cola for the road, a dignified pivot round the cones, and back to Tenby we wobbled.

Downhill should be a gift; after nearly ten hours it's an invoice. Each step detonated gently behind the kneecaps. I leaned forward in the style recommended by the competent and tried to relax, whereupon I instantly misjudged the camber, turned my foot and exclaimed, "Oh fudge!" A child materialised with an actual square of fudge. Tenby remains undefeated.

Re-entering town, the volume doubled. The odour of chips launched a hostile takeover of my will. Locals leaned from windows, waving dragons and slogans—SLAY THE DRAGON! KEEP GOING, BUTT! The harbour narrowed, the crowd pressed in, and the road became a pub aisle during a Six Nations match. Jelly Babies were thrust forth; I took a red one and confirmed sugar is a choking hazard. At mile five another aid station gifted me a Maurten gel which attached itself to my teeth like marital law.

We dipped under The Paragon arch—instant medieval courier— then turned left to the Esplanade where the sea glittered like a show-off and the headwind wrote rude letters to our dignity. My cap tried to emigrate. "That's uncalled for," I told the breeze. "Welcome to Wales!" said a passing stranger, fondly.

End of Esplanade, choose-your-own-adventure: straight to the finish (for people with four bands and a sense of closure) or right onto Picton Terrace (for the rest of us). A fluorescent marshal caught my gaze lingering longingly down the straight. "Not yet," she sang. "Three more loops." Polite brutality.

Right I went; short side street; up South Cliff; Lap Two: déjà vu, heavier.

Connie and the children were exactly where I'd asked them to be. Ellie filmed with one hand and waved with the other. Jack announced, helpfully, "You've only got to do that three more times!" Bella barked once and resumed being philosophically canine.

"You look better than Freddy!" Connie called. "He's only just ahead!" I offered a cracked grin. The moustache would be reckoned with later.

Lap Two mirrored Lap One, but under harsher lighting. The slope to New Hedges had added interest; aid stations had become carnivals; salt drew chalk maps on my arms. My stomach began to file strongly worded letters. I walked more, rebranding it "strategy." The taste in my mouth toggled between salty, sweet, and "sports drink regret."

Mind games unpacked properly. I counted (one hundred run, twenty walk), recited song lyrics (wrongly), and mentally listed every forbidden word for educational purposes. Light hallucinations drifted in: the hedge on my left was briefly a dragon that whispered "Gel?" Blink. It was, indeed, a gentleman in a dragon onesie offering gels. I accepted, because when life offers you myth with electrolytes, you nod.

"Band two!" cried the volunteer at New Hedges. I slid it beside the first and felt the wrist grow oddly momentous. Someone pressed a salted crisp into my palm. It tasted like absolution. The noise had intensified: chairs out, flasks up, a brass band gamely attempting "Delilah," small girls in national dress "Da iawn!"-ing with weaponised sweetness. I nearly wept; the wind took the blame.

Coming down Narberth Road my right foot sent a sharp communiqué up the shin. I slowed. Batman—cape aflutter—appeared, patted my shoulder, and said, "Dark times never last; Welsh support always does." Remarkably, it helped. The pain, affronted by optimism, subsided.

Halfway up the drag the trio re-emerged from a hedge like budget wildlife presenters. Baz narrated into his phone: "Observe the Midlife IRONMAN pretending this slope is fine." Kev contributed a life hack: "Pickle juice cures cramp. I don't have any—thought you should know." Dan walked parallel on the pavement, strictly outside the tape, and murmured, "Lamp post to lamp post. Bank it, bottle it." Then he exited before a marshal could invent a proximity clause.

Back in Tenby, the pubs had reached full belting volume. Pints were held over barriers like sacramental objects. A sign read SMILE IF YOU PEED IN YOUR WETSUIT; I complied. Another proclaimed PAIN IS JUST FRENCH FOR BREAD; I chose not to investigate. Under the arch again, onto the Esplanade again, the wind ratcheting up like a theatrical villain who's checked the running order.

Lap Three is where optimism is taken aside and spoken to firmly. Legs: lead. Stomach: brewing. Humour: stepped out for a little lie down. I felt filled with treacle and governed by bureaucracy. The official pattern set in: run, walk, cry, jog, repeat. Thirty seconds of earnest shuffling, a minute of dignified trudging to the accompaniment of mangled Hen Wlad Fy Nhadau, then a quiet pep talk and off we trot again. Somewhere between miles twelve and fourteen the foot niggle staged a coup; a blister I'd pretended not to know tore with operatic flair. "Oh, do behave," I said, a touch louder than intended. "All right?" asked a nearby runner. "Just my foot divorcing me," I said. "We're being very adult about it." She nodded. "Mine left at mile seven. We're friends."

The sun, which had previously minded its manners, removed its jacket. Clouds that had been chummy withdrew. Sweat upgraded to glaze; salt frosted my eyebrows. I licked my lips and got cola dust. Flies arrived to provide enrichment. Someone swatted and clipped another athlete. "Oi!" "Sorry!" Even camaraderie has bylaws.

The next aid station restored civilisation. Volunteers vogued to ABBA in wigs, distributing cold sponges like benedictions. I baptised my head, took cola, crisp and jelly babies, and shuffled on with the dignity of a damp duke.

Somewhere in Lap Three I misplaced Freddy on the mental map. He might have been ahead; he might have been behind; I had become a devotee of three metres of tarmac and the heels in front. Occasionally I lifted my head to admire hedgerows or sea, just to prove to myself I was not, in fact, on a treadmill in a shipping container.

Hallucinations made a proper bid for office. A man waved bacon rolls; upon approach he was a marshal with a sign: NO BACON HERE, BUT BEER AT THE FINISH. The tarmac produced jellyfish; they resolved into glittering gel wrappers. "Jellyfish," I whispered. "Hold your line." Reader, I did.

At mile sixteen, back in New Hedges, Band Three arrived with the gravitas of a knighthood. "You alright?" asked the volunteer, peering into my soul like an experienced GP. "This is fun," I lied with dignity. He handed me an orange slice. I bit and nearly applauded citrus as a concept.

IRONMAN Wales offers personal-needs bags on the run so you can stash the precise nonsense you'll crave: socks, Sudocrem, salt tabs, or a stern note from your past self. Mine contained all three plus a Mars bar labelled, in a moment of private theatre, YOU ARE A WIZARD, HARRY. At The Croft a volunteer called, "892?" "That's me!" I squeaked, like a man who's found his luggage. I sat on a kerb, peeled off a sock, allowed cold air to flirt with the blister, applied Sudocrem like a trench medic, and slid on the fresh sock with the reverence due to hosiery. Then the Mars bar—softened, heavenly. One bite and I was seven at a birthday party. "You are a wizard, Harry," I told myself. "You lot are insane," the volunteer said, very kindly. Both statements were correct.

The sugar rush lit a small, polite flame. Lap Four has a different weather system. Yes, legs cooked; stomach a cauldron of cola and banana; brain a soft white hiss. But the tunnel finally admits to a light. Mile twenty: "Single digits." Mile twenty-one: "Less than ten kilometres." Arithmetic became liturgy.

The last climb to New Hedges was both coronation and last rites. Every part of me filed complaints: feet—bricks in wet socks; hips—industrial action; shoulders—petitioning for better conditions. Mouth—coated in confectioner's regret. I longed for a toothbrush and a quiet life. Spectators sensed the endgame and doubled down. "It's your last one! Slay that dragon!" yelled a man in a straw hat. "Nearly there!" blared a woman with a megaphone powered, I assume, by hope. I wanted to hug them; alas, upper limbs had resigned without notice.

At mile 22.7 the final band was thrust forth. "Band four! Home straight! Bring it home!" Elastic slid over elastic; my wrist now weighed like a small, ridiculous crown. Posture lifted by a scandalous inch. "Thank you," I managed. He misted me with a water gun. "Cool down, champ." Reader, I would name a child after him.

Turning back toward Tenby, I glanced at the watch: twenty-three miles. Three to go—just under 5 km. The final chapter of the day belonged to those last streets: pain sharpened into meaning; joy elbowed in; hallucination kept things spicy; homecoming beckoned with a crooked finger.

The sky turned obligingly dusky pink. A courteous breeze touched salt on my face. Shoes slapped out their metronome; four rubber bands ticked on my wrist like an approving committee. I thought of strangers who'd turned every corner into a parliament of encouragement; of Connie and the children on the Esplanade; of Ellie's camera, Jack's bell, Bella's noble bemusement. I allowed myself one private, gentlemanly thought about Freddy's socks.

And then, with all the ceremony I could muster, I kept moving. One lamp post, then another. "Not long now," I told myself, as pleasantly as possible. "Just hold it together."

I looked up at the town that had shouted me into being brave. The noise swelled. I ran on to find the ending.

Chapter 27: The Finish: The Dragon's Tail

I left New Hedges with four elastic bands round my wrist and the weight of a small galaxy pressing on my shoulders. Each band was a receipt for suffering already paid in full. Four bands meant I was finally permitted to run straight at The Paragon instead of turning right for yet another lap of humiliation. Four bands meant the finish line had graduated from myth to geography. Four bands meant I had officially run out of excuses.

My head announced there were fewer than five kilometres left. My watch translated this as, "Thirty minutes, if you still possessed functioning limbs," which I did not. My legs had filed for industrial action, my stomach was curdling like cheese in a tumble-dryer, ...and my mouth tasted of cola, salt, and chemical courage. I was dry of tears but soaked in despair. Five kilometres: the shortest, longest, stupidest distance on earth.

A volunteer hollered after me, "Straight on at the arch, finish is waiting!" He said it with the manic cheer of a man who's repeated the line two thousand times but still believes in magic. I raised a trembling thumb in gratitude; all the other fingers had resigned.

Narberth Road rose like a petty bureaucrat—slowly, insistently, and with malice. The spectators could now read us like horoscopes. "LAST ONE!" they bellowed at the sight of my wristbands. "NO MORE NEW HEDGES FOR YOU!" Children thrust out sticky hands for high-fives; I managed a clammy brush that felt more like a health warning. Still, they cheered as though I'd liberated Wales.

The final aid station loomed, a fluorescent oasis promising salvation through carbohydrates. An IRONMAN official had once said, "Always eat and drink here, even if you don't want to; the last miles are a trap." I obeyed like a pilgrim. Cola—fizzy dynamite in my intestines. Two salted potato wedges—hope disguised as starch. A slice of orange—acidic truth that reignited nerve endings I'd forgotten existed. Then a sponge of cold water over my head: instant baptism. "Last sponge, love!" cried a woman in a fairy crown. I nodded; she was clearly my guardian angel.

As the body shrieked, the mind began its own radio drama. I pictured Connie scanning the crowd, Ellie filming my slow demise, Jack undoubtedly double-fisting hot-dogs, and Freddy—dear, cursed Freddy—perhaps stranded somewhere, debating between cola and crisps while maintaining that smug, water-resistant moustache. Once, beating Freddy had been the mission; now, I merely wished him gout. This was no longer man versus moustache. This was man versus himself—the bloke who once got winded chasing a bus and accidentally signed up for an IRONMAN while shopping for bin liners.

The climb crested, and Tenby's rooftops appeared, shimmering like a mirage made of mortgages. The noise swelled. A woman in a Welsh rugby jersey screamed, "COME ON, IAN!" For a second I thought she was psychic, then remembered my name was printed on my bib. Still—it felt divine.

The final 5 K of IRONMAN Wales is not a run; it's a pageant. And every pageant needs floats. Mine consisted of Dan in a bucket hat, Baz with two cowbells, and Kev leading a chant that contained exactly one lyric: "DAD NEVER FAILS!" They bounded along the pavement like overexcited Labradors, each one more lubricated by beer than the last.

"FREDDY'S MOUSTACHE IMPLODED AT MILE TWENTY-ONE!" Dan yelled.
"Allegedly!" added Baz, filming in case of lawsuits.

Re-entering Tenby felt like storming Wembley with the grace of a giraffe on stilts. The harbour roared; children waved flags; dogs barked encouragement. The chippy's vinegar fumes nearly triggered tears. Every step annotated with signs of motivational lunacy: YOU ARE STRONGER THAN YOU THINK! CARBS ARE COMING! YOUR NEARLY AN IRONAMN, BUT NOT YET. A small boy in a Spider-Man costume screamed, "YOU'RE WINNING!" which was factually inaccurate but emotionally appreciated.

My shuffle upgraded to a sort of noble jog as I turned by the harbour. The cobbles were ankle-assassins, but adrenaline temporarily issued diplomatic immunity. The streets had shrunk into an echoing tunnel of hysteria. Teenagers dressed as daffodils pounded drums. An elderly man in a deck chair nodded, mouthing, "Fair play," like a benevolent coroner.

Halfway along The Croft, my right calf cramped with the ferocity of a shark attack. I yelped and performed a spontaneous interpretive dance. A marshal lunged forward: "Stretch it! Stretch it!" I obliged with a grotesque parody of a yoga pose, the crowd applauding as if I'd reinvented balance. The spasm eased; dignity did not return. I hobbled onward, fuelled by embarrassment and the distant smell of beer.

At The Paragon arch, the familiar marshal stood like Saint Peter at the gates. He clocked my four bands and grinned. "Straight on, champ—the red carpet's yours." My heart squeezed somewhere behind the salt crust. Straight on. No more laps. Just destiny.

The Esplanade opened before me like a red-carpet premiere for idiots in Lycra. The famous crimson runway gleamed under floodlights, flanked by grandstands packed with screaming strangers and flags that flapped like applause. The white arch at the far end blinked my time with cruel honesty. The IRONMAN logo glowed like a deity demanding tribute.

I straightened my posture, zipped my tri-suit as if preparing for a royal audience, rotated my race belt so my number was visible, and quickened from "wounded mammal" to "determined wobble." The announcer's voice thundered across the promenade.

"And here he comes... from Porthcawl, Wales... he signed up because he was looking for bin liners... give it up for Ian Dawson!"

The crowd exploded. I laughed, then nearly choked on my own disbelief. Connie must have told them. My cheeks hurt from grinning. The timing mats beeped beneath my feet; my watch vibrated its final approval.

And then, over the roar and the lights, the words I'd rehearsed in my mind through every miserable training session finally arrived:

"IAN DAWSON, YOU ARE AN IRONMAN!"

The words hit like divine thunder in a gale of confetti. They say hearing you are an IRONMAN makes grown men weep; I can confirm it also makes them look like damp ferrets wrapped in tinfoil. I crossed the line in 15 hours, 47 minutes and 23 seconds—give or take the time it took my watch to decide I was still alive. I had done it. Somehow, through several acts of personal sabotage and at least three near-religious experiences, I was upright.

A volunteer materialised beside me like an angel in hi-vis. "You did it!" he shouted directly into my ear, though to me it sounded like whale song. Another volunteer draped a medal round my neck—solid, cold, and far heavier than my sense of achievement. I burst into tears, or possibly leaked electrolytes. A third helper wrapped me in a silver foil blanket that crackled like a bag of crisps. "Straight ahead for pasties and massage," she said with the calm authority of someone who'd seen too many Lycra-clad breakdowns.

I staggered forward through the finishing pen, a newborn giraffe wrapped in Bacofoil. Someone unclipped the timing chip from my ankle as softly as untying a shoelace on a sleeping child. At the refreshment table I faced a banquet that looked biblical: pizza slices, crisps, Welsh cakes, fruit, soup. I reached for pizza, chewed once, then realised I'd forgotten how to swallow. I settled for two cups of chicken broth, which restored both my humanity and my ability to blink.

At the massage tent I collapsed face-down, making a noise somewhere between a groan and a prayer. Two pairs of expert hands began kneading my legs as though testing dough. I whimpered, they called it recovery. Somewhere nearby a man snored mid-massage; another announced he'd lost feeling in his kneecaps and wasn't sure he wanted it back. Despite the pain, a serene fog settled. The dragon was dead. It had devoured my pride and several toenails, but I had slain it all the same.

I retrieved my street-clothes bag—a relic packed by an optimistic version of myself who believed socks were optional. I changed behind a flimsy curtain, wobbling like a baby penguin. The hoodie smelled faintly of home detergent; civilisation had never seemed so luxurious. Beside me another athlete examined his feet and murmured, "They're divorcing me, aren't they?" I nodded in solidarity.

Then I stepped outside.

***

The Esplanade shimmered under floodlights. Crowds still howled as finishers came through, each welcomed like royalty and roadkill combined. And there they were—my lot—Connie and the kids, front row behind the barrier. Ellie, phone in hand, documenting my ruin; Jack bouncing on the spot, brandishing two ice-cream sticks; Bella barking her moral support; Connie with open arms and that look halfway between pride and disbelief.

I staggered toward them. Ellie leaned over to photograph the moment before I could pose. Jack pointed to the medal. "Is it chocolate?" he asked. "No," I croaked, "but it should be." Connie hugged me so tightly my ribs reconsidered their alignment. "You're an IRONMAN," she whispered, equal parts awe and gentle mockery. "How do you feel?"

"Full of emotions," I said, the understatement of the century. Then we both laughed and, inevitably, cried—because apparently dehydration wasn't enough punishment.

Behind us the announcer roared another name; another poor soul achieved mythical status. The conveyor belt of triumph continued. I shuffled aside to let the next hero have their spotlight.

Moments later, the lads arrived like a travelling circus of idiocy. Baz ceremoniously produced a brand-new roll of bin liners and held it aloft like Excalibur. "For the sequel," he intoned. Dan handed me a printout of our WhatsApp thread titled The Bet—a masterpiece of broken promises and owed pints. Kev inspected the medal. "Looks edible," he said. Jack smirked. "He wishes."

We watched as more finishers poured down the red carpet: some sprinting, some collapsing, one deranged soul doing cartwheels. A man proposed to his partner; another waved a Welsh flag the size of a tent. Every few seconds the announcer declared, "YOU ARE AN IRONMAN!" and the crowd thundered it back like a national anthem for lunatics.

In that cacophony I felt a strange serenity. We were a fraternity of the unwise: mechanics, nurses, plumbers, accountants— ordinary mortals who'd paid good money to suffer publicly. Some looked heroic; others resembled ambulatory compost. But we'd all done the same ridiculous thing: swum through diesel, cycled up cliffs, and run until our souls detached. A man in a dragon onesie sporting four lap bands leaned over and said, "Not bad for a Sunday, eh?" "Next week," I replied, "I might mow the lawn." We both laughed until our abdominals threatened mutiny.

***

Later, sitting on the grassy bank overlooking the darkening sea, foil cape rustling in the breeze, medal resting like a paperweight on my chest, I traced the entire absurd journey back to its spark—the day I clicked Register while shopping for bin liners. That single idiotic click had blossomed into months of panic, porridge, and neoprene indignity. It had birthed Freddy, the pink-bag debacle, the jellyfish hallucinations, the hills, the near-religious moments with cola and crisps, and now this: peace.

IRONMAN Wales had proved itself exactly as promised—half battle, half festival, entirely mad. North Beach at dawn was equal parts hymn and horror. The locals were saints disguised as hecklers. St Bride's Hill and Heartbreak Hill were not climbs but trials of character. Even the zig-zags and the Esplanade had personalities—vindictive ones. And those final words, "You are an IRONMAN," were more than marketing; they were absolution for every foolish mile.

As darkness bled over the Pembrokeshire coast, Connie slipped her hand into mine. "You'll never do that again," she said. I nodded solemnly. Then she raised an eyebrow. "You said that after the half."

She was right. Beneath the ruin and salt and pain, some treacherous ember still glowed—the one that wondered whether lightning might strike twice, whether there might be another start line, another red carpet, another dragon to chase.

Perhaps not next year. Perhaps never. But then again... perhaps I'll open a cupboard, reach for the bin liners, and accidentally sign up all over again.

And honestly—wouldn't that be perfectly, stupidly, magnificently me?

Interlude: Night Thoughts

Lights out. Body very much on.

The medal's still round my neck, cold coin tapping my chest every time the calves scream. Not muttering — full choir. Left one cramps, right one joins in for harmony, both furious I made them descend that last hill like a newborn giraffe.

Connie's asleep diagonally, proper out, the way people sleep when they've carried half the day without any chip timings. Outside, Tenby finally shuts up — one last gull heckle, a door, then quiet. Inside, I'm a vending machine full of buzz. Every thought shakes loose and rattles.

I try the classic methods:

Close eyes and count sheep. Sheep turn into age-groupers and start overtaking me on Heartbreak Hill.

Breathe in fours. Works until the medal shifts and does the tiny clink that says You actually did it, and then I'm wide awake again, grinning like an idiot in the dark.

My legs keep firing phantom strides. Toes fizz. Hamstrings argue. Quads send an incident report titled: Immediate Restructure Required. I negotiate with them like a hostage taker. "We'll stretch tomorrow. We'll bathe in gravy. There will be roast potatoes." Calves remain unconvinced but agree to a ceasefire of thirty seconds.

The day keeps replaying in fragments, jump-cuts:

A marshal saying my name like we were old mates.

That corner in town where the rain went warm and the street smelled like chips and hope.

The moment — tiny, private — when I knew I was going to make it, and everything got quieter inside my head even while the world got louder.

The sentence from the finish keeps arriving on a loop — You. Are. An IRONMAN. — and every time it lands I feel the ridiculous prickle behind the eyes and have to stare at the ceiling like I'm checking for leaks. I'm buzzing. I am a power station with no grid to dump into.

Cramp ambush. Both calves seize like someone's yanked the handbrake. I grab the headboard, hiss obscene poetry, breathe through it like a man giving birth to two hot ferrets. It releases. I laugh. Quietly. Because it's funny — the pain, the joy, the sheer jackhammer aliveness of it. I didn't get fireworks at the finish. I got this: a night where being alive is loud.

The ribbon smells of rain and cola. Salt still on my eyelashes when I rub them. My hands remember the shape of the barrier tape, the high-fives, the cup that was Coke that was medicine that was rocket fuel.

I think about taking the medal off. I don't. Not tonight. Tonight it's part of the deal. The small knock of it when I breathe is a metronome for a year I didn't quite believe in until I crossed a bit of carpet.

Beside me, Connie rolls, finds my wrist, leaves her hand there like a receipt. "Sleep," she says without waking, as if it's something you can just choose. I try. The body hums. The brain screens today's highlights with director's commentary. Somewhere near three a.m., the calves calm to a sullen whisper and the medal cools flat against my chest.

I don't so much fall asleep as run out of awake.

PART 7: Re-Entry: Life After IRONMAN

Chapter 28: Recovery Roast

"IRONMAN isn't just a day, it's a medical condition."
I woke in the B&B feeling like I'd borrowed a stranger's body and forgotten the return policy. Occupying a body I didn't recognise — parts missing, warranty void. Muscles I'd never met had left passive-aggressive notes. The quads, last seen screaming up Heartbreak Hill, had downgraded to a continuous disgruntled hum; shoulders felt as if a marching band had used them for warm-ups; feet were two microwaved balloons; even the ears had opinions. Raising my head required coalition talks. Rolling out of bed demanded a full risk assessment and a waiver.

The medal still hung round my neck because I insisted on sleeping with it—romance isn't dead, merely limping. At 3 a.m. I woke with the M-dot embossed on my cheek like a cattle brand for idiots. I smiled at the thought and instantly regretted it; apparently I'd installed lactic acid in my dimples. I tottered to the bathroom. My ankles clicked like castanets. Sitting on the loo produced a sound somewhere between a sigh and a kettle just before boil. I briefly considered establishing residency there; the return journey looked ambitious.

Downstairs smelled of bacon and coffee—civilisation's two most persuasive arguments. Connie was up, the children were semi-vertical, Bella was auditioning to be a chainsaw. I descended the staircase clinging to the banister like a Victorian heroine. My family looked up, equal parts concern and entertainment.

"How's the IRONMAN this morning?" Connie asked, sliding coffee towards me with A&E tenderness.

"Please don't make me laugh," I croaked. "My ribs and ears hurt."

Ellie didn't look up. "Let's also not make him breathe, Mum. Looks precarious." She scrolled. "Your finish-line video has eight thousand views. Someone slowed it down and added dramatic strings. Comment of the day: 'Like a sloth crossing the M4.'"

After breakfast we attempted the outside staircase to the street. Yesterday: an afterthought. Today: the Hillary Step with added heckling. I descended performing new, exploratory lunges. Connie shadowed me like a spotter at a human zoo. A fellow finisher in compression socks bounded past with gazelle grace. "Morning!" he chirped. I wished him a light yet instructional cramp.

Tenby was rubbing the sleep from its eyes. Banners still flapped; the red carpet was already a memory. Volunteers stacked barriers with supernatural cheer; shops restocked; locals nodded at hobbling athletes with that special respect reserved for people who've done something both daft and vaguely noble. Outside a bakery my calf staged a coup; I grabbed the sill and performed a calf stretch that read as experimental dance. A baker emerged with Welsh cakes. "Fuel?" she offered. Butter, sugar, kindness. "Best crowd in the world," I mumbled through crumbs. She nodded. "We love our Ironmen. The atmosphere's something special."

***

The plan—carbs, friends, and a pub carvery—was simple and, somewhere between miles 18 and 20 yesterday, erotic. Connie booked a table at a roast-forward establishment and summoned our people. It turns out when you survive an IRONMAN, acquaintances wish to view you in daylight to confirm rumours.

En route we passed medal-wearers with the haunted cheerfulness of survivors. Ten-second debriefs bloomed: "How was your swim?" "Lost goggles at buoy two." "Bike?" "Dropped chain at Wiseman's." "Run?" A pause. "Let's never speak of it." We laughed, winced, shuffled on.

The pub, hugging the town wall like it had witnessed things, already buzzed. IRONMAN hoodies everywhere; faces still the shade of unrisen dough. The bar staff wore "Recovery Fuel Specialists" shirts, which felt both accurate and enabling. Our long wooden table faced a window like a jury box. Friends arrived bearing hugs, high fives and crackling mockery.

Tom and Sarah from the running club appeared first. Tom clapped my shoulder. "He lives!"

"Barely," I said, moving as if underwater.

Neighbour Dave arrived with his wife and a cake shaped like the M-dot—heroically proportioned, faintly menacing. "Told you I'd bake something if you survived," he said. It looked capable of feeding ten Ironmen and a small choir. "We may need to check whether this counts as carbo-loading," I said, eyes dilated.

***

The roasts arrived like cavalry. Thick slices of beef, pork crackling snapping like twigs, the sort of chicken skin that causes arguments. Roasted potatoes in offensive quantities, Yorkshire puddings the size of millinery, gravy by the jug— medicinal. Bowls of carrots, green beans, cauliflower cheese circulated like a secular communion. Connie had arranged extra potatoes. "He needs them," she told the server, accurately.

I constructed a geological formation and told the nutrition police in my head to take the day off. The first bite of beef made my eyes water. Gravy tasted like absolution. The Yorkshire was a soft architectural miracle. Someone parked a pint at my elbow; it bloomed on the tongue like spring. "If this is heaven," I said, "their marketing's been underselling it."

Between mouthfuls, I obliged the table with Greatest Hits: the zig-zag sprint in a wetsuit clutching a pink bag; Welsh grandmas advising me to relocate my backside at mile eight; the split-second realisation at The Croft that I was finally going straight; the audio of 2,000 swimmers politely attempting not to remove one another's goggles; jelly babies adhered to my molars for twenty miles; the gel-on-bike moment I tried to swallow dignity and nearly returned it to sender. Sarah snorted cider when I reached the bacon-roll hallucination on Narberth Road.

Observers filled in the broadcast side. "At one point the commentators said, 'Here comes Ian, plodding along,'" Tom intoned in his posh voice. "Plodding!"

"I plodded like a champion," I said through potato. "Plodding was my superpower."

Ellie, our embedded media desk, updated metrics. "Mum's finish-line post has three hundred comments. Aunt June says you need your head examined. My friend Daisy says you're hot." I inhaled a Yorkshire and had to be re-gravitied.

***

Plates cleared, Tom adopted an orator's face. "We have prepared something." Oh no. Sarah struck her glass with a wooden spoon, the international signal for theatrical humiliation. Faces turned, eyes twinkled.

"As is traditional in our club," Tom announced, "we now deliver the Recovery Roast. Not the edible one—the character assassination. It is how we show love."

I covered my face. "Please be gentle."

"We shall be accurate," Sarah said. "First, the moustache."

Uproar. Tom continued. "Never has one man been so haunted by another man's upper lip. Freddy, if you can hear us, thank you for your villainy. Ian's moustache envy got him up Heartbreak Hill faster than physics allowed."

They moved to aquatic matters. "Ian trained for months and still swam like a man wrestling a duvet in a wind tunnel," Tom said. "At one point he appeared to head for Ireland. Coastguard confirmed a yellow-capped figure doing interpretive cartography."

On the bike, Sarah relived my chain-drop. "He rehearsed mechanicals, then reinvented sculpture. A small child on a tricycle shouted, 'Pedal, you cabbage,' and Ian briefly considered hiring him."

Nutrition followed. "Yesterday he ingested six bags of orange slices, three gels, two bananas, a Welsh cake from a mystic stranger and, at mile 74, his dignity," Sarah read. "We're astonished he didn't request gravy at the feed station."

Finally, the run. Tom spread his arms. "He ran, walked, cried, jogged and hallucinated his way around Pembrokeshire. He survived jelly-baby dentistry, ABBA at 11.7 miles, and at mile 18 declared himself a wizard."

They raised glasses. "To Ian," Tom concluded, "the only man who can register for an IRONMAN while shopping for bin liners—and finish it. Our plodding hero."

I laughed until my abdomen lodged a complaint and my eyes leaked again. To be roasted like that means your people were watching, filing away your idiocies with care. It felt, in its way, larger than the medal.

***

As the roast potatoes retreated and cake advanced, conversation turned technical in that alarming endurance-athlete way. We discussed chafe creams like oenophiles. Compared salt tablets. Debated whether Saundersfoot's wind was a head-tail conspiracy. Forensics on pacing and T1s would've impressed the CID. Dave leaned in. "Be honest—did quitting ever flirt?"

"Yes," I said. "On the bike, chain off on an incline, fingertips Jackson Pollocked with grease—thought, 'What am I doing?' Again at mile 21 when a blister detonated and I hallucinated deli items. But each time I pictured the months, the bin-liner impulse, your faces in Tenby—and thought: if I stop now, I'll only have to come back. Better to finish once than re-sit the exam."

Connie squeezed my knee. "Good. Because if you'd quit I'd have registered you again out of principle." The table applauded policy-based love.

Recovery is peculiar. The body begs for calories; the stomach stages theatre. I dipped a roast potato in gravy and then apple sauce—culinarily sinful, spiritually correct. Cake happened at speed. Taste returned in Dolby Atmos. Each chew felt like applause.

My phone buzzed without ceasing: colleagues, estranged cousins, people who once beat me at rounders. Boss: "Take the week, IRONMAN. Please also limp through the workshop next Monday for morale." Mum left a voicemail: "I watched you finish, cried, told next-door you were mad. Proud of you. Shed roof?" I promised the shed a modest rebuild.

A man in civic jewellery (mayor or enthusiastic cosplayer) toured the pub shaking hands, IRONMAN tee beneath his chain. "Well done, all. You've terrified the locals and filled the B&Bs." We toasted the patron saint of organised disruption.

The next day brought awards and world-champs slots at the De Valence. I had zero illusions; my time placed me between "respectable" and "ornamental." Still, curiosity demanded attendance. The hall thrummed with people who looked capable of starting again for fun. Age-group winners bounded on stage, teeth and times gleaming. Sub-nines for pros, sub-elevens for civilians: biology's show-off cousins. We clapped like well-brought-up furniture.

Slot allocation turned the room electric. A woman behind us whispered, "Missed by three minutes," and gripped her partner's hand as if time could be reverse-squeezed. Tears—some of joy, some of arithmetic. For some, the finish line is merely an interval. For me, it was a full stop with exclamation. I clapped for the Kona-bound and the sofa-bound equally.

***

Logistics beckoned: collect bike and bags. The seafront car park looked eerie, as if the circus had vanished overnight. Racks mostly empty; the odd orphaned elastic still fluttering. A volunteer handed me blue and red bags. "Please check your belongings." I nodded sternly at each relic. Wetsuit: pungent, accounted for. Bike shoes: unrepentant, present. Helmet: stoic. All went into the boot like captured flags.

***

By evening the adrenaline had exited through the gift shop. Fatigue threw a blanket over me. Back at the B&B I lay on the bed watching the ceiling attempt to turn into the Tenby skyline. My brain played a private montage—anthem at dawn; diesel and salt; hedges, hills, and holy lunacy; the red carpet—and set it to orchestral percussion. I startled awake at one point convinced I'd missed a cutoff. Connie stroked my hair. "You finished," she whispered. "You're safe."

DOMS peaked forty-eight hours later: stairs remained cursed architecture. Sleep arrived in neat parcels, punctured by dreams of swimming uphill. Appetite: biblical. I texted Tom—"Is it normal to want to eat my bodyweight in custard?"
"Yes," he replied. "And if you're still hungry, eat the spoon."

Messages kept arriving. Someone from school wrote: "Didn't expect the lad who faked asthma to dodge cross-country to do an IRONMAN. Legendary." I laughed, coughed, then laughed at the coughing. Weeks later I'd catch the medal winking from the wardrobe and smile like a fool with receipts.

***

If IRONMAN taught me anything, it's that very few finish lines are solo signatures. Connie absorbed early alarms and late sulks. Ellie and Jack produced propaganda and noise. Friends rode, swapped gels, and heckled me into competence. Volunteers—faces I'll never properly remember, voices I'll never forget—navigated us with "Stay left, butt!" and "Straight on, champ!" The town itself was a character: Tenby, patron saint of poor decisions performed bravely.

The Recovery Roast proved it's not just about replenishing glycogen; it's communal processing. Translating ordeal into anecdote. Mocking the catastrophe into meaning. Admitting frailty, applauding stubbornness. Community doesn't clock off when the timing mat stops beeping.

***

That evening, after we'd eaten too much and said we'd never do this again with suspicious sincerity, Connie suggested a stroll along the Esplanade. The sky was painted in competently executed pastels. My legs attempted several excuses; my heart overruled them. We shuffled past the ghost of the finish—red carpet gone, a faint pink echo on the tarmac like lipstick on a glass. Flags still muttered. Two teenagers on the wall shared chips and gossip, spotted my quartet of band marks and gave a thumbs-up as if approving a building inspection.

"I can't believe it's over," I said, watching the sea that had tried to eat me now pretending innocence. "Was it yesterday? Last week? Hard to tell."

Connie threaded her arm through mine. "You turned it back into a memory," she said. "That's the trick—do the impossible, then fold it small enough to carry."

We stood and listened to the tide behave itself. Everything hurt, but my chest felt very light. In the distance, the zig-zag traced the cliff like a private joke. I thought of the pink bag, the anthem, the daftness and the courage, and felt that quiet, treacherous ember flicker—the one that wonders what else might be possible.

Connie squeezed my hand. "Come on, IRONMAN. Bed."

Chapter 29: The Tattoo

In the quiet days after IRONMAN Wales—once the swelling had retreated like a tide and I could descend stairs without whimpering like a haunted kettle—the question that had been loitering at the fringes marched to the centre and cleared its throat. Do I do it? Do I join the inked tribe? Do I mark my leg with a corporate hieroglyph so permanently that future grandchildren will point at my calf and ask, "Grandad, why is your leg sponsored?"

If you've spent more than five minutes around triathletes (I don't recommend more), you'll notice a curious zoological marker: they are branded. Ankles, calves, shoulders—each bearing the same sacred glyph, the M-dot. Some are discreet as a whisper; others shout from a quadriceps like a billboard outside a motorway services. Occasionally the dot sprouts flames, dragons, coordinates, offspring, and a full family tree. It's a badge of honour, a souvenir, a lifetime membership to a club that never meets but always nods knowingly at airports. The internet hosts fierce debates: "It's a commercial logo!" "It's my body, my saga!" "I've earned it!" "It's ghastly!" The comment sections require goggles.

During those early recovery days, I swan-dived down a warren of blogs and forums about tri tattoos. A former pro declared triathlon and tattoos practically inseparable; for many, their tattoo story and triathlon story are plaited like a friendship bracelet. A gear guide assured me the classic M-dot lives on the calf, loudly signalling strength and endurance—a popular way to commemorate one of the world's most needlessly difficult days. A rite of passage, apparently, like learning to parallel park or admitting you enjoy beetroot.

Why was I entertaining this? I'm not a tattoo person. I didn't cross the finish line and shout, "Fetch the needles!" I boast a skin portfolio consisting of a freckle and some poor moisturising choices. Yet the thought of carrying a permanent talisman—

equal parts pain and perseverance—had an allure. Also, peer pressure is a dreadful cheerleader. In our club chat, Sarah posted her husband's ankle with a tasteful, smug dot. Tom wrote, "Ian, it's compulsory." Dave sent a meme of a calf the size of Anglesey, emblazoned with an M-dot and the caption: "In case anyone missed that I was an idiot once." Ellie forwarded a TikTok: Reasons to get an IRONMAN tattoo: 1) Because you can. 2) Because your kids will think you're important enough to interrogate at school.

Connie remained magnificently Switzerland. "It's your leg," she said. "If you want one, get one. If you don't, don't." I adored her neutrality. She did add, gently, "If you get Freddy's moustache tattooed anywhere, I shall rebrand myself as single."

I drew up a spreadsheet. Pro: conversation starter at dull gatherings. Con: yes, a logo. Pro: octogenarian me might gaze at it and think, "Once, you were brave or at least unsupervised." Con: my calves are more "two reluctant scones" than "Michelangelo." Pro: a permanent reminder that a misclick while shopping for bin liners led, via disaster, to the red carpet. Con: needles. I am not needle-forward.

In the end, logic slunk off and feeling took the wheel. On day three, I caught my four lap bands still hugging my wrist—grubby, frayed, smelling faintly of achievement and sports drink. I could have slipped them off, but hadn't; they were my paper shield. In a week they'd perish; the medal would collect dust; memories would blur. A tattoo, though—stubborn as a biscuit tin. I wanted something that would make me smile and wince and whisper "Heartbreak Hill" like a curse and a prayer. A small piece of Tenby I could take to the supermarket. A nod to the ridiculous pledge I'd made the night I searched for bin liners and instead bought life choices. I texted Tom: "Book a consultation before I regain sense."

Decision made, the serious dithering began. IRONMAN tattoos are a buffet. Do you go classic M-dot? Do you twine a Welsh dragon because Tenby has annexed your ventricles? Date? Time? Coordinates? A cheeky moustache (divorce court says hello)? Subtle or "hello from across the bay"? Tri folk have turned the M-dot into a stained-glass window.

I scrolled galleries. Minimalist thumbprints; full-leg frescoes featuring every race an athlete has ever terrorised. The research did more than fill a Pinterest board; it inducted me into the tradition. On Smashfest Queen, the writer practically married her ink to her sport; the two stories were one. Elsewhere, the M-dot's popularity was framed as a totem of strength and endurance—a durable souvenir of an undurable day. Reading, I felt less lemming, more pilgrim choosing his cairn.

Placement? The calf is standard: visible with shorts, vanishes under trousers, adjacent to the miles you bribed your legs to cover. Ankles for the discreet; arms, chest or ribs for the confident or masochistic. The calf felt right—chief engine for St Bride's and Heartbreak Hill, and occasionally cooperative.

Style, then. I didn't want "just the dot"; I wanted a footnote. I doodled: a dragon curling round the M; Tenby harbour with spectators the size of lentils; a moustache atop the dot (struck down by the domestic courts). I sent sketches to Tom. His replies: "That dragon is a seahorse." "Absolutely not the moustache." "Keep it simple; you can always vandalise yourself later."

Connie reviewed and laughed precisely once—at the moustache. We converged: classic M-dot, event date, and a small Welsh dragon curled at the base like a guardian. No moustaches. No bin liners. No pint glasses (tempting).

***

Selecting an artist felt like choosing a surgeon with better playlists. This was permanent; I require neither regret nor cartoon dragon. Tom recommended a Cardiff studio specialising in endurance athletes—"They're used to trembly middle-aged men." Sarah floated Swansea for fine-line witchcraft. Dave, cake architect, said, "See Jay in town. Did my rugby crest. Genius. Loves IRONMAN."

Google yielded Jay Ink—Jason to HMRC—whose studio, "Ink & Anchor," lurked off a side street near the harbour. His portfolio: clean, bold, clever. Many an IRONMAN—red dots with waves, bikes, dragons, even Celtic knots swaddling the logo. Reviews fawned over his listening and storycraft. Sold. Appointment booked.

***

A tattoo studio is a dentist with better art and worse small talk. Antiseptic in the air, machines humming like domesticated hornets, the tacit knowledge that discomfort equals souvenir. Ink & Anchor was compact and welcoming: walls ablaze with anchors, roses, portraits, and a polite scattering of M-dots. A record player murmured classic rock; it soothed my cowardice. Jay—tall, sleeves of art, backwards cap—grinned and shook my hand.

"So, IRONMAN?" he said. "Congratulations. Tenby, right? Glorious punishment."

"Yes," I said. "I've been told Wales will revoke my visiting rights if I don't acquire the official stamp."

He laughed. "Some circles do treat arriving un-inked like wearing shorts to a wedding."
I showed him my doodles. He nodded, confiscated the moustache with the air of a disappointed art teacher, and asked, "Colour or black?"

"Colour," I said. "Red dot, black dragon. The flag, but subtle."

He sketched—swift, confident. In minutes: a bold red M-dot, the dot generous enough to sprout a subtle swirl from which a sleek dragon tail curled beneath the M, head peeking out like a watchful cat. Underneath, neat date. He mischievously added "Never Again (Maybe)" in pencil. We removed the cheek, kept the date.

Connie studied it. "It's you," she said. "It's Wales. It's not dreadful."

"Let's do it," I said, and my stomach executed a neat backflip.

***

Tattoo pain is an eccentric relative. People describe it as cat scratches, sunburn sketching, electrical nettles. I had only memories of diesel flavoured seawater and the sensation of my soul vacating on Heartbreak Hill.

I lay on the leather chaise, calf propped, courage prodded. Jay explained: outline, colour, shading. He prepped the skin, placed the stencil—there it was, my future mistake or masterpiece. The machine buzzed. "Ready?" he asked, I nodded.

First contact: a bite, sharp as impoliteness. Then the brain did its translation: persistent scratch, warm thrum, tolerable ache. Unpleasant? Yes. Unbearable? We've met worse. I inhaled. Connie squeezed my hand and filmed, already writing the caption: "From bin liners to ink liners."

We chatted. He'd inked dozens of Ironfolk. "Sometimes they arrive the morning after, medals on," he said. "I send them home. Immune systems have to choose their battles." He liked the tradition: "It's a medal you can't lose in a sock drawer."

I recounted Tenby: the anthem at dawn, the pink-bag peloton, Freddy's moustache lurking in my psyche, a child consultant yelling "Pedal, you cabbage!" Jay laughed so hard he lifted the needle to safeguard straight lines. "I'm using 'cabbage' on my kids."

As the outline emerged, my mind wandered to sensory postcards: the taste of salt and faint diesel, the jellyfish/plastic-bag diplomacy, the aquatic kick to the goggles, the chorus of "Da iawn!" at New Hedges, the carnival at Saundersfoot, the red carpet's ridiculous magnificence. The machine's buzz became white noise, like a wheel on smooth tarmac.

Half-time needle change; my calf thrummed. Connie offered a jelly baby; I declined on medical grounds (trauma). Phone buzz: Kev—"Please get Freddy's moustache on the dragon." I typed, "Cease." He replied, "Live-stream the pain."

Colour time. The red laid down with a sting and a whisper. I thought about permanence. There are so few 100% decisions:

finishing an IRONMAN is one—you cannot un-swim nor un-run it. Ink is another. Both require the odd bargain with discomfort, both give you back a thing you didn't have before: a story you can point at. Mid-life crisis, but tasteful.

Jay wiped away ink and the metallic shade of effort, then held up a mirror. There it was: the red M-dot, dragon

curled like a sentinel, date below in modest script: "15 September 2024." The skin around it blushed; the design sat there, oddly inevitable. Pride arrived with a giggle. Corporate logo plus mythical reptile now part of my anatomy. It looked great. It looked absurd. It looked like me.

***

Jay wrapped the fresh artwork in cling film and issued commandments. "Clean with unscented soap, pat dry, thin ointment, no soaking or sun, no picking. It will itch. Do not audition for the itchiest." It read like a training plan penned by a school nurse. Connie nodded, committing it to the maternal archive. "Like a newborn," she said. "Feed, clean, shade, no strangers poking it."

We stepped into cool afternoon. My calf tingled—tough and tender at once. At a café I rolled up my trouser leg for the ceremonial reveal. Ellie filmed; Jack squinted. When we unwrapped it later to wash, the colours popped. "That's brilliant," Ellie pronounced. Jack nodded, solemn. "The dragon's guarding treasure. Is Freddy getting one?" "Only if there's a salon for moustaches," I said.

I posted to the club: I have joined the cult. Sarah: "Welcome, brother." Tom: "Excellent. Where's the moustache?" Dave: "May the dragon breathe up Heartbreak next time." Boss: "Shorts at work require HR briefings."

Beyond the bubble, reactions varied. Mum: "You've vandalised yourself! What if they change the logo?" "Then I'm vintage," I said. Neighbour Pat: "Lovely mermaid," she said, and I questioned both our eyes. At the school gate, a parent said, "My cousin had to choose—tattoo or another IRONMAN. He chose the second." We nodded in the reverent silence reserved for dangerous romantics.

Unexpectedly, the supermarket became a lodge. I was reaching for flour when a stranger clocked my calf. "Tenby?" he asked. I nodded. He hitched his trouser to reveal a weathered M-dot: "2014." We chatted about wind, course tweaks, and the superior feed-station snacks like veterans comparing campaigns. The tattoos were passports; the world briefly shrank to a village where everyone had once tried to out-swim jelly.

***

In the end, the ink wasn't a boast; it was a bracket closing. The IRONMAN arc began with bin liners, detoured through disgrace, training, Tenby's lunacy, and a red carpet that felt like theatre. The tattoo was a period. "It happened. It mattered. It is mine." When I look at my calf, I don't just see a logo; I see a tamed dragon nodding to a town that shouted me home. I see a date, proof I was, on that day, the version of myself I'd doubted existed. And, faintly, I see the ghost of a moustache I did not include, and it makes me laugh.

Will there be more ink? Possibly. Another IRONMAN? Ask me when my stairs no longer require a Sherpa. For now I have a dragon-guarded M-dot, four fading band marks on my wrist, and a story that started with bin liners and ended with a pleasantly menacing buzz and a permanent souvenir.

Chapter 30: Thoughts: Reflections and Last Confessions

There's a peculiar limbo between finishing an IRONMAN and rejoining civilisation. For days after Tenby I floated about as if the world were upholstered—fog, pillows, and occasional cutlery. My legs alternated between "cast-iron radiators" and "loaners from a scarecrow." My appetite went feral and began writing its own shopping lists. Sleep arrived in oddly shaped parcels, as though my body refused to accept that 5 a.m. hill repeats were no longer compulsory. I could ascend stairs without issuing a formal complaint, but every so often my calf twitched and—hello again—there was the little dragon inked upon it, a scaly post-it note reminding me what I'd done.

At some point in every triathlete's saga, a sensible person asks, "Why?" Fair question. Why volunteer for pre-dawn nausea? Why choose rain over Netflix? Why spend unholy hours astride a turbo, staring at a wall crack like it's an art installation? Why pay handsomely to swim in chilly soup, cycle until your thighs file for legal separation, and then run a marathon on legs that have turned to inexpensive lumber? Why flirt with the exquisite humiliation of missing cutoffs? I'd asked myself all of that before Tenby and produced respectable answers: to prove something to myself, to get less squishy, to fend off midlife beige. True enough. But the day itself delivered footnotes in large print.

First discovery: suffering and joy are twins who share a bank account. Those grim little moments—being tenderised by the surf, bargaining with gravity on Heartbreak, trudging the final lap with a face like a tax audit—were welded to the ecstatic bits. I will henceforth taste sea salt and hear the anthem at dawn. The burn at Wiseman's will always carry the echo of "C'MON, BUTT!" from a stranger who meant it. Joy wasn't the absence of discomfort; it was the cheeky grin you manage while sitting directly in it. The hardest bits produced the best stories. The internally polite swear-moments are exactly the ones I recount most often, because that is when I felt gloriously, absurdly alive. You don't get one without the other.

Second discovery: I am not the only cheerful lunatic. Train mostly alone and you begin to suspect you're the sole idiot with a spreadsheet. Then you reach Tenby and find two thousand other spreadsheets in trainers. Even in training, community kept popping out from hedges. An elderly couple on a long ride handed me hosepipe water like nectar and announced they'd cheered Wales for years. A pool stranger swapped bike routes as if we were trading recipes. Old schoolmates surfaced to wish luck. Volunteers materialised by the thousand to clap, point, and prevent us from doing anything irreparably foolish. I'd assumed endurance sport was selfish. It's not. It's deeply communal theatre. Your private grit only goes so far; the roar of strangers will lug you up a hill when your internal monologue has packed up and gone home. One sticky high-five from a kid trumped an entire packet of gels.

***

When I clicked "Register," the word "athlete" felt like cosplay. Knees too creaky, lungs too vintage. Training had other ideas. Turns out the body, when bribed with snacks and light bullying, adapts. Muscles show up late but eventually clock in. Heart rates learn manners. Swimming drifts from "elegant drowning" to something approaching rhythm. Climbing stops being a cry for help and becomes a chat with your gears. Running off the bike remains the sport of "why am I like this?" but, somehow, grows normal.

I learned I can ride 112 miles without my backside quitting the company. I learned I can jog on broom-handle legs. I learned that one can, at 30 kph, eat a peanut-butter sandwich and not make the local paper.

More surprising was the brain under pressure. It's not a temple; it's a travelling circus. One ring houses a drill sergeant: "Push. Again." Another hosts a therapist: "Breathe. Lovely. Continue." A heckler roams the aisles muttering, "What are we doing, you absolute muppet?"

During the swim, my brain wrote sea shanties and a grocery list (forgot the milk). On the bike, it recited a roast recipe (lost the gravy). On the run, it became a market trader: "Reach the feed station and you may walk for thirty seconds."

The trick, I learned, is scale. 140.6 miles is monstrous; the next five is doable. A marathon is mythic; the next lamppost is manageable. The brain learns to shrink chaos into chunks it can chew. And, for the first time in a long time, I started to think— maybe that lesson works outside Lycra too.

***

Tenby, bless it, is not just a postcard; it's a stage. For one glorious weekend the town becomes open-air opera. Flags everywhere. The harbour wall thrumming. People leaning from windows banging saucepans like percussionists on overtime. Children with inflatable clappers tolling them like bells. The athlete guide promised the support was world-class; for once, the brochure undersold it. Locals who've seen every edition still shred their throats. Visitors who didn't know triathlon from trigonometry roar like seasoned ultras. Teenagers in dragon onesies perform interpretive encouragement. Toddlers, bubbles, and nose-glitter cheer as if it pays. Volunteers in hi-vis spend seventeen hours distributing sponges, cups, and unreasonably sincere eye contact.

The course? Half postcard, half personality test. Narberth Road, New Hedges, The Croft, The Paragon—these names now live rent-free in my hippocampus. Saundersfoot? That's not a hill, it's a lifestyle choice. Heartbreak Hill felt like being cheered up a volcano by people who'd had too much Red Bull. Tenby itself turned medieval—walls closing in, streets roaring, air thick with sweat, chips, and misplaced encouragement. Even the descents judged me. Every climb whispered, you signed up for this, and every corner replied, you idiot. Pastel houses, medieval arches, town walls, a tunnel of joyful noise. The loops are genius and cruel: you meet the same crowd four times. On lap one they're tantalising (yes, we smell the chips too). By lap three they're practically family: they know your name, your gait, your band count, and your tendency to accept jelly babies and poor decisions. The moment you finally skip the Picton Terrace purgatory and go straight to the carpet is—no exaggeration—a sensory thunderclap. Lights. Music. The announcer's theatre. A word you thought belonged to other people. I will not forget it.

***

If you're flirting with something gloriously daft, here are my entirely unscientific notes. Start where you are, not where your imagination has photoshopped you. I began with rebellious goggles and a 25 m pool. Running for more than fifteen seconds was ambitious. Early progress is invisible; continue anyway. Next: chunk everything. A marathon is simply a necklace of aid stations. A bike ride is villages stitched together by questionable tarmac. A swim is strokes between buoys and the occasional jellyfish negotiation. Practise transitions; yes, really. They are small, silly, and matter. Acquire a respectful relationship with zips. Find your people—the supportive noise is not garnish; it's fuel. And keep your why somewhere visible. It will go missing at 5 a.m. You'll need to wave it under your own nose.

Will I do another full? Ask me in a year. Presently I oscillate between "Never again" and "Possibly Bolton if bribed with roast potatoes." Memory is a charming liar; pain fades, glory keeps a scrapbook. But my ego has been fed; there's nothing left to prove. Perhaps a 70.3. Perhaps parkruns and smug coffee. Perhaps knitting. Perhaps a podcast—Bin Liners & Bike Chains. What I do know: I want to keep moving, attempting silly valiant things, and telling stories about the mess. Triathlon turned the volume up; silence now seems impolite.

***

If you've trudged along with me—from the bin-liner mis-click through the training pratfalls, Abersoch's moustachioed haunting, Tenby's hysteria, and all the puddles between—thank you. If something scares you, poke it. It needn't be an IRONMAN. It might be a 5 k, a dance class, a novel draft, French subjunctives, or phoning the person you miss. Do the thing. Expect it to be inconvenient, scruffy, and occasionally full of self-doubt. Expect, also, to meet the kinder bits of yourself and other people. There will be jelly babies. There will be saucepans. There will be someone in fancy dress who says exactly what you need, precisely when you need it.

If you do choose IRONMAN Wales, a few public service announcements: the hills are steep, the sheep refuse to care, and the seagulls are thieves with wings. The crowd will carry you; the volunteers will finesse your survival; the red carpet will take liberties with your tear ducts. You will be called an IRONMAN even if you feel like a malfunctioning shopping trolley. You will cross a line and not be quite the same as the anxious creature who entered. You may, if taste permits, acquire a dragon on your leg.

I'll finish with this. At my absolute nadir on the run, a lad of about eight yelled, "Don't stop! You'll regret it forever!" Not the sage I expected, but the prophet I received. He was right. The regret of stopping would have weighed more than the pain of continuing. Whether or not I ever string together 140.6 again, I'll carry that line into future nonsense: Don't stop. You'll regret it forever. Unless it's a 5 a.m. alarm. In which case, a single snooze is practically medicinal.

Thank you, Tenby. Thank you, IRONMAN. And, of course, thank you, bin liners.

15th September
2024

About the Authors

Darren Gibbons

Darren writes because he's survived it. His field notes are half triumph, half "what was I thinking?"

His philosophy is simple: consistency beats talent, humour deflates ego. He's finished multiple IRONMAN events, discovered that chafing is the tax on enthusiasm, and learned that progress comes from patience, not punishment.

When he's not training, coaching, or writing, he's writing, coaching, and training. He also maintains a spreadsheet called MASTER PLAN v23-final-FINAL and still believes this time it really is.

He was proud to ask Alan Adye-Rowe to join him on this book— if Michael Jackson is the King of Pop, Alan is the King of Race Reports. Darren brings the chaos; Alan brings the chronology. Between them, triathlon becomes three sports and one long punchline, stitched together and powered by early alarms, long runs, and a frankly irresponsible number of Jaffa Cakes.

This book is powered by Darren's own experiments, missteps, and glorious downfalls—every wrong turn, dodgy gel, and "this'll be fine" that absolutely wasn't. Some scenes are practically eyewitness accounts. Could parts of Ian be Darren? You decide. And if your GPS file ever looks like a spider on espresso, welcome—you're in the right book.

Alan Adye-Rowe

Alan hails from the sun-soaked chaos of Durban, South Africa — where rugby is religion and sunscreen is more of a rumour. After nearly two decades in New Zealand, he developed a confusing set of sporting loyalties and an accent that alarms airport security. He now lives in Herefordshire, surrounded by polite hedges and a climate that treats sunshine as gossip.

Once a keen sportsman, Alan spent the next few decades taking an extended break to focus on snacks and denial. A health scare in 2023 prompted what motivational speakers call "a wake-up call" and what Alan calls "a rather aggressive reminder that time waits for no man — except possibly one in compression socks."

Since then, he has hurled himself into triathlon — an activity combining three disciplines he's yet to master, at a cost that could fund a reliable used car. He's survived Long Course Weekend Wales, IRONMAN Swansea, and IRONMAN Weymouth, with finish times measured exclusively by sundial.

He trains under Smart Performance Coaching, whose patience has now been certified as saintly. His family are his loyal support crew — dispensing jelly babies, sarcasm, and the occasional reminder to put his tri-suit on the right way round.

Alan was genuinely honoured (and mildly bewildered) to be asked by Darren to help bring Ian's story to life — a tale so close to his own that parts of it may in fact be confessional evidence.

He remains proudly unqualified to give fitness advice but entirely qualified to deliver cautionary tales. His philosophy is simple: you don't need to be fast, fearless, or particularly gifted — just stubborn enough to start and too stupid to stop.

www.ingramcontent.com/pod-product-compliance
Lightning Source LLC
Chambersburg PA
CBHW070910130626
46555CB00001B/76